HISTORY OF JUJU MUSIC

**A HISTORY OF
AN AFRICAN
POPULAR MUSIC
FROM NIGERIA**

T. Ajayi Thomas

HISTORY OF JUJU MUSIC

...from the one-man band of minstrels like Togo Lawson and Irewolede Denge 1920s and 1930s, to the four-man combo of Tunde King 1930s and 1940s, to the twenty-two piece band of Shina Peters 1990s, Juju has come a long way.

HISTORY
OF JUJU MUSIC

A HISTORY OF AN AFRICAN POPULAR MUSIC FROM NIGERIA

T. AJAYI THOMAS

ILLUSTRATED
THOMAS ORGANIZATION-SHADE LABEL-FISHER MUSIC

THOMAS ORGANIZATION
NEW YORK, U.S.A.

HISTORY OF JUJU MUSIC

*This book is dedicated to my children, Ayorinde, Oluwatoyin,
Adeyinka, Adenike, and Bankole; my sisters, Shade Thomas and
Iyabo Atta; all my nephews, nieces and the rest of my sisters.*

FIRST EDITION
Copyright © 1992
T. Ajayi Thomas
P. O. Box 641
Jamaica, NY 11431 U.S.A.

Manufactured in the United States of America.
Published by T. Ajayi Thomas - Thomas Organization

Library of Congress Catalog Card Number 92-90780
International Standard Book Number 0-9633261-0-4

Printed in the United States of America

CONTENTS   Pages

ILLUSTRATIONS

ILLUSTRATIONS

ILLUSTRATIONS

Sango (*Oba Koso*)

A Yoruba man
The Yorubas are famous for their tribal marks, a custom that is no
more in practice these days.

Yoruba women
The Yoruba women with their colorful and flambouyant attires are
unbeatable in matters of merriment and jollity.

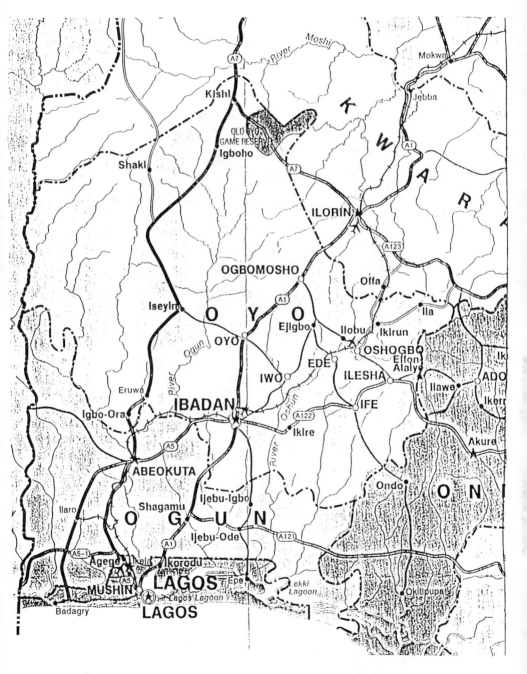

Sectional map of Nigeria showing Ife, Oyo and Lagos.

Sanusi Yusuf, Chief Aromire of Lagos, the great grandson of Aromire who was the first to establish real estate in Lagos and who was also one of the thirty-two children of Olofin, the Yoruba indigene from Ile-Ife who inhabited Lagos around 1400-1500.

ACKNOWLEDGEMENTS

The popularity of Juju music internationally has made it impossible for its history to be ignored.

Sunk deep and clustered with countless of various Nigerian music types, a great deal of effort with scrupulous care has to be exercised in nailing down facts in an attempt to bring it out since looseness cannot be tolerated when dealing with historical subjects.

Acquaintances and deep personal contacts with principals involved, true stories of old Lagos handed down by sages, octogenarians, old close relatives and family members, intense research work in books from public libraries, text books, and personal experiences all contributed in the writing of HISTORY OF JUJU MUSIC.

It is now a cliche when writers take an opportunity in some few lines to thank various helping hands that have contributed in bringing their books out to the market; but which other known ways could they have shown their appreciation better? Appreciating the artworks that my wife Norma, an artist, did in the book and giving thanks to her is an understatement. She labored day and night even when she was not in a good mood, on illustrations that are in the book, some through sheer description and some through photographs to bring perception and accuracy to the subjects.

Neil DeGennaro, Vice President and head of the production department of Doremus & Company, the company that did the initial typesetting of the book, is the source that should not be left unmentioned. The go-ahead signal from him paved the way for bringing out this book because without his authorization, the typesetters would not have touched the script.

Raymond Cruz, Fran Andresen, Megan Huddleston, Lou Lombardi, Joe Morgan, Mike LeBourveau and most especially Gary Williams whose accuracy in typesetting is uncanny, all have another of my vote of thanks; and also Simone Conigliaro the mechanical artist who did a lot of the paste-up work.

And damn if I forget Pa. Ayorinde Thomas my father, (may his soul rest in peace) who settled in Lagos from Oyo sometime after the formative stages of Lagos and who was able to furnish me with authentic stories of pre and Colonial days of Lagos, from the Okokomaiko train and Akintoye Baba, the Ebute Elefun assassin to Lady Santos and the obaship of Lagos disputes. Quips and punchlines about Lagos's old days ricochetting off his lips always sent listeners rollicking and rolling off their rockers.

And lastly, a word of advice. Never throw away old books and pictures. Keep them! When I graduated from elementary and high schools in Lagos, a lot of my text books and some other informative books about West Africa and the colonial days were discarded. Two decades later and one thousand four hundred miles away from home, by some strange coincidence I was at a place where some old books were to be thrown away. Upon close inspection, some of these books happened to have rings of nostalgia to them and this time the same mistake was not allowed to be repeated. Tropical Hygiene by E. J. Evans 1924, which I used for my hygiene studies in my fifth year at elementary school, Introduction to West Africa published by His Majesty's Stationery Office London 1948, which I have read as a toddler in my elementary school days and General Science by Sutcliffe Canham Chapman which was my text-book in science in my secondary school days at Baptist Academy, Lagos, as a teenager were all staring me in the face. I grabbed them all and this time kept them. Believe it or not, they helped in the writing of History of Juju Music. Also two DRUM magazines of the 1960s that I have acquired for keep's sake all of a sudden became a great source of information in one of the A WHOLE SCENE GOING topic in this book and some pictures in the magazines also were really Godsend. Being in music too, a lot of the musicians mentioned in the book whom I have personally met and discussed with and some who are great friends of mine, furnished me with valuable informations which I greatly appreciated.

Some events that occurred at the same time with juju get passing mention in the book but are later isolated and separately treated in a topic called A Whole Scene Going. This is necessary because some readers may be curious to know of these events but since dealing with them in details with juju may cause deviation in the history of the music even though the events are germane to the main subject, they are isolated and given full treatment separately to satisfy the readers' curiosity. A Whole Scene Going simply means a lot of things happening at the same time.

History of Juju Music is not only meant for music enthusiasts and or for reading pleasure; being historical, it could also be used as a text book in schools and colleges for courses in history and music. Thank you everybody.

THE AUTHOR

T. Ajayi Thomas was born in Lagos, Nigeria. Attended Christ Church Cathedral School (Faji) Lagos (kindergarten), St. Peter's School (Faji) Lagos and Ereko Methodist School Lagos (elementary), Baptist Academy Lagos and Awe High School (Awe) Oyo (secondary). Worked as a journalist for the Daily Express, Lagos, in the early sixties and left Nigeria for further studies overseas just after the Nigeria independence.

Attended Norwood Technical College London, England and graduated in science (Biology-Parasitology) at St. John's University, New York, U.S.A.

He became involved with music during his youth days when he started to play the trumpet. As a composer, arranger, singer and bandleader, he has made quite a number of singles and about ten LP records. He plays all kinds of music. In addition to being a scientist and musician, he also writes television plays and movie scripts.

Says the Author: "Writing *this book, History of Juju Music, is an especially satisfying project for me. Indeed very nostalgic. It takes me back in time to my youth days in Lagos, where I was born and to the street where I was reared. I was born at 8 Odunfa Street, Lagos, some five hundred yards from Evans Street where Togo Lawson was born. I knew Togo very well and have trailed his tracks some few yards listening to some of his songs like* Awa O Sise. *I have seen him pounded the tambourine competently to accompany his songs. Although slightly eccentric, he was a jolly good fellow. What made him so amiable was his love for kiddies and that was why I liked him. Irewolede Denge was special but different. I knew him too, up close and personal. He first lived at Oshodi Street and then moved to Ije near Obalende before he died of throat problems at the General Hospital, Marina, Lagos. Whenever he came around in the night singing and accompanied by the framed rectangularly shaped samba drum, I have ran out of the house to listen to him and to follow him some few yards. As years went by and around the 1940s, my first time of seeing young Tunde King was in a live performance at Tokunboh Street and Akanbi Ege at Igbosere Road. I was one of the pupils of Christ Church Cathedral School (Faji) Lagos, who sang his nationally popular song against Hitler that went: "HITILA TIN D'AIYE RU O, E FAGARA TI SI KOTO O." (Hitler who is causing confusion throughout the world, use the shovel to dump him in the grave). I have enjoyed Meu-boi Meu-boi. I have participated in fancy, caretta, sailors and egun oniko (raffia masquerade). I have enjoyed asiko, parade, conga and konkoma types of music. As a musician myself, I met and have known a lot of African musicians; highlife and juju artists most especially. I knew the foundation and growth of western influenced music in Nigeria. Tunde Nightingale, bless his soul. I was around him with Ade Bashorun to console him as despondency got the better of him when he was stranded in London in the 1960s. I have recorded on the label that the great Ambrose Campbell recorded on and coming back to interview the likes of Tunde King, Dele Ojo, etc., etc., and meeting with leaders in the music like Sunny Ade, Ebenezer Obey, etc., have been wonderful experiences for me.*

There are many reasons for writing this book but only five need be mentioned. (1) A lot of people in Nigeria today, could, with a great deal of bounce and swagger tell everything about Mozart, Beethoven, Chopin and Tchaikovsky including the type of food they had for breakfast on the day they wrote their first concertos but ask these people who Tunde King is or Alabi Labilu. One will be extremely lucky, if, with a taint of sarcasm they do not answer back with Tunde who? or Alabi who?; whereas these are the people they should first have known something about. (2) No doubt, western education was one of the great civilizing influence on Africa but it has been discovered that today, there are some people born and bred in Nigeria but who could not speak a word of any of the Nigerian vernacular languages. They converse with people in English as if it is their mother tongue. This is western education "run-a-mock" and the ridiculousness of it cannot be overstated. (3) Some music players today make good money and live a good life. This is good. But it is also good that these players should know the lives of the people of whom the fruits of labor they are enjoying because nothing comes easy. (4) We have lost our "endangered species" and we have made the mistake of not making recorded history. The herbs that our forefathers used to cure ailments before the arrival of western health programs if properly recorded and improved upon would today have put Africa on the vanguard of medicine and related health programs but instead our western education had made us to derisively and variously call this ogun, vileness, ignorance, juju, voodoo, black magic etc., and we have lost our respect; to give just an instance. We should never allow this mistake to be repeated. (5) The Nigeria of today is certainly different from the Nigeria of past years; but how can our children know that Nigerian coinage once included onini, epinni, kobo, toro, sisi, and silekan let alone cowrie which never was minted. Four oninis were one epinni (one half-a-penny). Two epinnis were one kobo (one penny). Three kobos were one toro (threepence). Two toros were one sisi (sixpence). Two sisis were silekan (one shilling). Twenty silekans were pounkan (one pound sterling) and pounkan silekan were one guinea (one pound one). Onini, epinni, kobo and toro were all minted in silver steel. Sisi and silekan were gold colored steel minted. Pounkan was in paper form. Also silemewa (ten shillings) was in paper form. As for cowries, they can be found today as decorations on the attires of worshippers of Sango, the god of thunder and lightning. Now, how about "owo Ijebu"? (counterfeit money). Believe it or not, most of these coins where counterfeited and spent to buy merchandise from unsuspecting dealers. Why were these counterfeit money named after Ijebu town? Well, the Ijebu people were ingenious. The first set of people caught with the machine that manufactured these counterfeit coins were probably the Ijebu townfolks; hence the name. How do we explain to the youngsters that in the old days during some special holidays, there were street celebrations known as Meu-boi Meu-boi and groups such as fancy, caretta, sailors, fanti, cowboys and egun oniko that jollify some other street festivals? How does one describe oro, egungun, gelede, alapafuja etc., etc.? A pinch of salt would have to be added to get youngsters of today to accept the fact that in the old days, one can walk from morning till night without being molested in Lagos and that when youngsters have from epinni to toro in their pockets, they were considered rich. A naira couldn't buy much today but one could get a pocketful of guguru (popcorn) for one onini in the old days not to talk about epa and agbon (peanuts and coconuts) that the seller will sprinkle on one's guguru as a "dash" for patronage. Those were the days.

It is really astonishing to me to find juju music, out of all the other types of music in Nigeria, gaining international prominence. Highlife music, because of its western influence was the music that I thought would have made it but there you are. As they say "You never know."

INTRODUCTION

Thousands of horns may sound from dawn till dusk giving beautiful melody and harmony, what they cannot detract from is their basic attribute of listening pleasure. Once there is an incorporation of rhythm through drums or sticks into these horns, mood changes, atmosphere also changes. The drum is a stimulant. It has the power to excite, to initiate movement and to carry out different kinds of mood in humans. It is medicinal and has been used from time before recorded history by Africans to drive out evil spirits, to prepare medicinal potions and to embellish incantations etc., etc.

Drums, rhythm and the element of timing all draw their origins from Africa. With countless of books on the topic of music floating on bookstores and markets all over the world, very few have given this credit to Africa. The same fate is suffered by African musicians, entertainers and writers. They are just not respected. The sway that the western world hold over the art industry is so immeasurable that it afforded it the arrogance of power never before seen in any other industry of equal stature. Three quarters of the book written on Africa are written by non-Africans. African music played and recorded by non-Africans find better markets than music recorded by Africans. Grants and funds are easily and readily available to any non-African who would like to take a fling at anything African but not so with real Africans. It seems as if everybody knows everything about Africa but the Africans themselves.

When research on anything African is made, sources of information are always from the ever generous Africans yet it does not seem to occur to these so called "authorities" on Africa that what made them what they are were the knowledge they acquired from the "inept" Africans. What logic can one draw from the following: In 1979 or thereabouts in the city of New York, a casting was being made for a film that required a part of an African diplomat. When advertisement was made, among people that showed up for audition were a Nigerian actor and a non-African entertainer. The non-African was picked to play the part. Here we are, the real thing was staring the producer in the face but he simply refused to see. The story however did not end there but took an amusing twist. The Nigerian was then hired to teach the non-African how an African diplomat naturally and professionally usually behaves! But if one thinks that the story has finally ended, well, not so. In the space of four days that the Nigerian took to give the lessons, he was paid $250 (two hundred and fifty dollars) with a promise of an invitation to the premier opening of the film in the theatre in New York. For a two week shooting of the film, the actor who played the part of the African diplomat was paid $2,500 (two-thousand five hundred dollars)!

This book, HISTORY OF JUJU MUSIC, was scheduled to be in the market by the Spring of 1987, but just could not make it because of many factors. After grants were unable to be obtained to finance its publication, proposals were then sent out to many publishing companies. They were all met with rejections. Subsidy oriented publishing companies were then turned to but their prices and royalty contracts were outrageous. University publications both in England and America were all consulted, none was interested. Here we go again. An African who was in the know and very ready to give authentic and first hand information on a popular African subject offered his services but was met with blatant rejections. When out of sheer frustration, I decided to privately and personally fund the publication of this book through the advice of a friend, members of my family rallied round me and pitched in, in any way they could, to help.

How can I ever forget my sister Shade Thomas Fahm of the Shade's Boutique fame. She supplied a large part of my transportation by freely allowing me to use one of her cars plus asking her driver to drive me to wherever I wanted to go. Not only that, during the time that I was trying to find additional materials to support most of the stories in the book, she always made sure that I was properly fed before leaving home in the morning and also at all times to feel comfortable too. At times, her concern about my safety and health in the city of Lagos where I was born bordered on craziness. She introduced me to the Republic of Benin, the former country of Dahomey's Ambassador, His Excellency, Hon. Patrice Houngavou who made my journey to Benin possible to video-tape and also to take pictures of the waters of Bights of Benin and some other historical places in the Republic. Another of my sister, Mrs. Iyabo Atta made a lasting impression that raised a family's pride. After reading the book, she was so impressed with the story and the general outlook of the book that for a while she ignored her tight schedule to give me moral and financial support in order to get some additional materials needed for the publication of the book. Adejoke Caulcrick another of my sister, contributed to the book with the memories of her childhood days at Odunfa Street in Lagos where she met personally with the early players of juju music.

And how about my nephews and nieces. They came out in droves to help in any way they could. Paul Adegbola Thomas took off a week from work to drive me around Lagos, Ibadan and some other towns in Nigeria in order to meet with some juju players and to take pictures.

I am indeed thankful to Akinlabi Thomas-Adegbola, another of my nephew who resides in Ibadan. For three weeks, he left his family to follow me about and to furnish me with tid-bits of what should be included in the book. One of the people outside of my family whom I can never forget for the help he rendered to me on this book is a gentleman and a personal friend by the name of Joseph Olajoyegbe Fajimolu, known easily for his recording label acronym of JOFABRO. He was the one who made it possible for me to meet again with Alhadji Abudurafiu Babatunde King, popularly known as Tunde King, now in his eighties whom I thought had died. He was the old king of juju music. We met twice and I had a long interview with him which was video-taped. He also signed some papers for me giving me the rights to use any of his records and recordings for my purpose. I first saw the old man in performance at Tokunboh Street in Lagos in the mid 1940s when he was a young man leading his group and rendering his services at a social occasion. He was either in conversation or argument with somebody and I can never forget the contact microphone attached to the "jakan" of his agbada by his chest and very close to his mouth to amplify his voice. That day, I didn't realize that the next time I would be meeting with him again would be in another thirty to forty years.

Back to Jofabro, I am also grateful to him for furnishing me with information on ANGARD. I am thankful to Papa O.A.L. Araba and his wife known affectionately as "Mama Sabo" who furnished me with a host of old records on the labels of Zonophone, Angard, HMV and others.

It was depressing to find the Nigeria of today looking like a fortress besieged. The Nigerian Naira is at its lowest of twelve Naira (N12) to an American dollar ($1) and N16 to the British pound sterling (£1).

One cannot take a picture or make a video-tape recording on a camcorder in the public without attracting attention of curious onlookers or the army or police officers. The police and soldiers are everywhere and they react first before asking questions. I must have taken over five hundred pictures some germane to the topic of this book, some for personal use. But while taking these pictures, of some nasty experiences that I had, two would never leave my memory. Because of the historical significance of Badagry in connection with the juju music, I decided to go there and take some pictures. My sister Shade, gave me her red colored Mercedes Benz car to use and loaned me her driver Lanre to drive me there. Upon arriving at the town, we missed our first subject to be photographed. After about fifteen minutes of searching we decided to ask a traffic policeman for directions. His direction led us back to where we had driven past and still we could not find what we wanted. Eventually, I decided to take the picture of a round-about of which four roads branched off--one westward, leading to Idiroko through traffic to the Republic of Benin, the former country of Dahomey; one eastward leading to Badagry Grammar School; one northward, leading to Badagry township and one southward, leading to Lagos through which we entered the town. As I got out of the car with my camera and snapped this roundabout, instantly two young army officers whom I had not noticed by the roundabout arrested me. They wanted to know where I came from, why I was taking pictures and how many pictures I have taken so far. What I didn't realize was that immediately we drove into the historic town of Badagry, our red Mercedes Benz car had been spotted and it had stirred curiosity. I introduced myself to them as a Nigerian, a Yoruba, born in Lagos but at that time residing in New York in America. I explained to them the purpose of the picture taking and I told them that I had taken only one picture so far. They refused to be satisfied. The interrogation continued with threats of severe penalties but I refused to panic or yield from my original honest intention that brought me to the town to take pictures. All of a sudden, in a bizarre twist, the more elderly looking one of the two soldiers fixed his eyes on me sternly, grinned widely and said "Gee!, I know you. Now I remember you very well. Three months ago at Alagbon Close in Lagos, you were arrested for doing exactly the same thing. Your camera was confiscated and you were thrown into jail for three months." Now, one would think that in my present predicament the farthest thing on my face would be a smile but not so. I found the comments of this soldier so risible, I thundered into a terrific laughter because I arrived back in Nigeria from the U.S. only two weeks before that day and even though I knew Alagbon Close very well, since my arrival back in town I have not been there. When I explained this to this soldier, he was disappointed that his seemingly good catch had escaped. "A nice try but not good enough", I murmured to myself. The younger soldier then took over. His interrogation was a dressed-down grilling that was unnerving in nature and ridiculous in motive. He decided to follow me to the laboratory in Lagos so as to have my camera opened and to have the film processed. Poor Lanre, my sister's driver. He was constantly exhibiting that Nigerian grin of frustration plus the constant shaking of the head.

The Badagry roundabout

Since I have become suspicious of these frauds in battledress, I told the soldier to sit in the front seat of the car with Lanre while I sat at the back alone because should in case he decided to pull a stunt, I would be at an advantage to stop him right there in his tracks. By now, the two soldiers have realized that I was not going to offer them anything to appease the situation because they have known all along that I was telling the truth. As the younger soldier opened the door of the car and made an attempt to sit, the other one then said to him "Let them go. He's probably telling the truth." To my surprise, the younger soldier stopped, backed out and asked me to go. I looked at the two of them and said "You still don't believe that I'm a Nigerian right? Anyway, S'alafia ni? Awon iyawo yin nko ati awon omo? E bami ma ki won." (These are formal Yoruba greetings asking about conditions of health, children and wives.) To these, they chuckled. I stretched my hands out to the two of them. We shook hands, and I entered the car. When I got back into the car, I told Lanre to let us get the hell out of the place fast. We did. Why not anyway, it was already dark and check-points were to be contented with before getting home. It was an unnerving experience for me. I was burnt-out by the time we arrived home. I just went straight to bed.

The Iju Waterworks building

The other nasty experience was at Iju, on the outskirts of the city of Lagos. To support my story of the Eleko Affair (*The Iju Waterworks*), I decided to go to Iju and to take the picture of the plant that works the Lagos's pipeborne water--*The Waterworks*. Upon our arrival there, I got out of the car and took two pictures of the front of the building. It was my luckiest move because I never got around to take anymore. As I finished taking the pictures of the building's frontal part, I entered the car and was driven to the gate. The gate was opened and the car was allowed in. I got out again and approached the sentry to tell him of my intentions. He was amused and asked me to see the clerk at the information desk who told me that he had no power to allow me to take the picture of the plant but would put me in touch with his superior. He called his superior on the phone and gave the telephone to me to speak to him. When I explained my intentions to this superior, he implored me to get out of the place as fast as I could because such a move would be in my best interest. When I asked why, he said that there were soldiers guarding the plant and they shoot to kill. He said that I would already be dead before they realized that I was an innocent man and that they would do anything to cover-up their mistake. I said to him that it probably would be appropriate to write to the head of The

Waterworks beforehand for a picture taking request but he said that it would be a waste of time because the request would not be granted. He then asked me if I had taken any pictures at all and when I replied positively, he asked me to leave the place that very minute because the soldiers would be on their way to the gate. And he terminated the conversation. I hurried into the car and we drove off.

Half of the hundreds of pictures I took by myself were modern or rebuilt places of where historical events took place and this is why I am immeasurably grateful to the Daily Times of Lagos whose staff supplied me with a lot of pictures of old to support my stories. There are also two people I should never forget to mention even if what is left in the pages of this book is one line. My fund was dwindling and this was compounded by a freak personal problem when my friend Charles Adichie Bobmanuel, owner of the Upwest Recording Studio stretched his hand out to help me to the fullest. He did all the recordings pertaining to this project for me, some free of charge, some on credit and also took personal care of me. I can never forget him. The other person is George Lamboy, introduced to me by Charles. George is the owner director of Regal Entertainment, Co., a Cable TV show and Video production company. Upon learning of my financial predicament and personal problems, George went out of his way and spent hours and hours of his time to edit for me on credit the video on the History of Juju music. Putting the story together from the many video tapes on which the story and scenes were recorded was a task of immense proportions but George withstood the challenge with enthusiasm. Thank you George.

This book is divided into three parts. Part one starts with a short story of the foundation and growth of Lagos. No one can write about the history of juju music and leave out the foundation and growth of the city. They were interwoven as could be seen in Chapters 1 and 2. Important and historical events that happened in Lagos also became important in the music's history because some songs memorializing these events were recorded with the sound of this music. In Africa, music is not just played for dancing and listening pleasure; it is also recorded to memorialize events. News of an event that appears in newspapers is geared towards the section of the public that can read. In time the shock wears off as news of other events take over and the papers turn their attention somewhere else. That same event's news can be carried on broadcast systems for a day or two and again attention is then turned elsewhere; but with a recorded song of this event, everybody, young or old knows about it as the disc is played time and again at home and at all sorts of gathering be it social or otherwise. Moreover generation after generation will be constantly kept informed of this event through this record. In this wise, juju music has done a tremendous job. Chapter 2 is devoted to the Missionaries who inadvertently, brought the instrument that was used to start the music. Chapter 3 deals with native medicine, a source of which juju music was thought to have derived its name. New events were used in this chapter to make some points in the discussion of old events. However, part one ends in Chapter 8 to round off the old ways of playing the music. Part two starts off with Chapter 9 that tells of modern juju music after the World War II and ends up with current juju music players on Chapter 12. Some of these Chapters have Sub-chapters bearing their own full topics. Part three encompasses Milestones, Special Mention and Chronology.

Note: A video, CD (compact disc), cassette, and record accompany this book in three packages of (1) Book, Video and CD, (2) Book, Video and Cassette, and (3) Book, Video and Record. All the materials in the three packages can be bought separately or individually.

HISTORY OF JUJU MUSIC

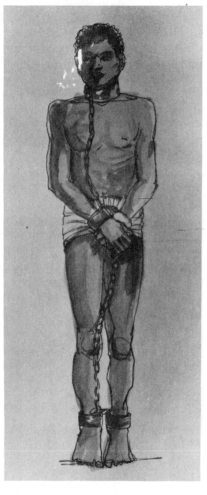

1

LAGOS

ILE-IFE (Ife) •
YORUBA •
OLOFIN •
SLAVE TRADE •

S ANGO "oba koso"(*the king does not hang*), the god of thunder and
lightning, the fourth king of Oyo in Yorubaland in the 4th century,was
probably the most famous of the Yorubas. Relatively less known was
ODUDUWA, the founder of the Yoruba tribal people who originated
from Ile-Ife the spiritual and ancient town of the Yorubas, not far from
Oyo, in the Yoruba heartland of the western part of Nigeria. Around
1400–1500, a Yoruba indigene, an inhabitant of Ife, by the name of
Olofin, left the town and migrated 120 miles east-northward to Lagos.
There, with thirty-two of his children, he settled permanently. Having
distributed the Lagos land amongst only ten of his thirty-two children,
one of his sons Aromire who was a farmer, used part of his land for
housing development and became the first person to establish real estate

in Lagos. However, as time passed and as development and advancement came, contest for the throne of Lagos became an issue that resulted in wars. Slavery, one of the end-products of the wars turned out to be a problem that stretched far beyond the realm of Lagos, brought it world-wide attention, and changed it socially. Lagos, situated on the coast of Gulf of Guinea in the South Atlantic Ocean, was a port of call of the Portuguese traders. Although Hanno, the third century Cartagenian statesman, sailed along the coast of Africa's Western "bulge" 300 years B.C., it was not until the Portuguese followed suite 500 years later that Europe received first hand accounts of the mysteries and riches of the unknown continent. Gold, diamond, ivory, and various spices discovered by the Portuguese in unlimited quantities were things that Europe was ready to pay heavy prices for and so began a frenzied trading race to Africa. To regulate trade with the various African tribes of the coastal belt, the Portuguese set up trading stations and for the protection of the trading stations, castles were built.

ELMINA castle in Ghana, today, is a good and reminding example. Because of the abundance of tobacco, sugar and cotton, and few people to harvest them on the plantation in America, slaves became a necessity and by the 1590s, other nations like the Dutch were attracted to West Africa because of "black" ivory. Rivalry in shipping black men from their homeland to be sold, continued for about 150 years until the humanitarian movement in England in 1807 put an end to it by making slave trading by British subjects illegal. Even though the British government had made it illegal for the British, what about the non-British? What about the African kings that were selling their own subjects? Would these kings have continued in such act if the fate of their sold subjects been disclosed to them? What about those who still wanted slaves for their plantation? And what about the traders who knew the cruelty meted to the slaves but had no moral compunction in shipping them?

It first seemed as if the problem could not be eradicated until it became an issue that divided Britain into pro and anti-slavery factions. The anti-slavery faction won their point and culminated in the Royal Navy setting up patrols along the West African coast during the next 60 years to suppress the inhuman trade which was then branded obnoxious and illegal. But the trade yielded so much profit that many dealers were ready to take the risk and to continue in it. In the 1860s however, the civil war and the abolition of slavery in the United States of America finally destroyed the demand.

In 40 years, from 1891, the Mixed Commissioner's Court of Freetown condemned over 500 slave-ships brought in by the Navy and liberated 57,000 slaves. The abolitionists had two very good

An old print of Elmina Castle in Ghana

pieces of luck on their sides. The second will be dealt with first. Necessity, the mother of invention plunged Britain into Industrial Revolution. This brought about increase in population. Most of all, nearly every invention brought about by the Revolution came with it its agents of discomfort of dust, slurge, slime, and grim which became a gigantic sanitary problem that the country had to cope with. Soap was needed and also a demand for candles, cooking oil and lubricating oil. These demands could be met by palm oil from West Africa and so a profitable substitute was found for trade in slaves. The first luck of the abolitionists came seven years prior to 1860 and it was this that signalled the birth of JUJU music.

Between 1851 and 1852, Lagos as usual was embroiled in the battle for its kingship. The reigning king, Akintoye the 1 was in a deadly fight against his uncle Prince Kosoko who wanted the throne. Temporarily chased out of his palace, the king went to Fernando Po to seek the assistance of the British who at that time was all over the West Coast of Africa waging war against the slave traders. John Beecroft who at that time was the British Consul in the Bights of Benin and Biafra, obliged, since it was an opportunity for him to expand the British fight against slavery.

With superior weapons including cannons, he despatched a detachment of British troops commanded by Commodore Henry W. Bruce to Lagos. Akintoye's men, with the British troops on their side, back in Lagos, restarted the battle in earnest. Red hot cannonballs discharged from the cannons and claiming victims in large numbers were what the Lagosians had never experienced before. The noise of the cannon, and the bubbly nature of the shell–fire made the Lagosians to name the battle OGUN AHOYAYA meaning the Boiling Battle. (*see Ogun Ahoyaya in A WHOLE SCENE GOING on Page 19*) Soon, the battle was over in the defeat of Kosoko and also his exile.

After the war the British signed a treaty with Lagos abolishing slavery. The treaty contained nine articles. Article number 8 was the one that signalled the birth of juju music. (*see Page 17 for Article number 8*).

The treaty with Lagos on January 1, 1852, opened the way for the arrival of missionaries in Lagos. The missionaries brought the religion of Christianity to Lagos which was accompanied by music played with the tambourine and other musical instruments. The pioneers of juju music started off the music with tambourine but without a name to it. It was years later that the music was christened "juju". After the treaty, the British gained a foothold in Lagos. In September of 1853, Akintoye died.

In 1853, Dosunmu (written Docemo by the British), Akintoye's son ascended the throne of Lagos. Because of the help that the British gave to his father in regaining the throne of Lagos, he was persuaded to cede Lagos to Britain. On August 6, 1861, he did and Lagos became a British colony.

The treaty with Dosunmu on the cession of Lagos to Britain contained 3 articles that brought problems which future generations of Nigerians had to deal with for years to come. (*For the three articles of the treaty see Pages 25 and 26.*)

Article 1 gave away the Lagosians' rights to the natural resources of their land. Article two devalued the title and prestige of the Lagos kings. They no longer could be called kings and article three took away not only the rights of the citizens and obas to landed properties but made the obas to be treated as salaried workers.

The innocent and illiterate king was probably ill advised and did not comprehend the broader implications of the treaty but four decades later, the colonial government started to have problems.

Meanwhile, both France and Germany entered the field of African exploration and at the Berlin Conference of 1884, the freedom of navigation on the Niger and Congo rivers were safeguarded by international agreement. At the same time, the general basis of what came to be known as the "Partition of Africa" was laid down. It amounted to this: that the claims of any one power to a particular part of the coast where its interest were predominant, together with such parts of the interior as that power could effectively control, would be recognized by the others. Under these rules, the British had a clear claim to what are now the coast lines of the Gambia, Sierra Leone, the Gold Coast and Nigeria. By devoting considerable energy to the interior, the French linked their own coastal possession by a continuous interior occupation. The four British territories were thus converted into enclaves without scope for further enlargements. By 1900 the frontiers had become stabilized. The white man's administration had come to Africa.

Following is Article Number Eight:

Article VIII

Complete protection shall be afforded to Missionaries or Ministers of the Gospel of whatever nation or country following their vocation of spreading the knowledge and doctrines of Christianity and extending the benefits or civilization within the territory of the Oba and Chiefs of Lagos.

Encouragement shall be given to such missionaries or ministers in the pursuits of industry, in building houses for their residence, and schools and chapels. They shall not be hindered or molested in their endeavors to teach the doctrines of Christianity to all persons willing and desirous to be taught; nor shall any subject of the Oba and Chiefs of Lagos who may embrace the Christian faith be, on the account, or on account of the teaching or exercise therefor, molested or troubled in any manner whatsoever.

The Oba and chiefs of Lagos further agree to set apart a piece of land, within a convenient distance of the principal towns, to be used as a burial-ground for Christian persons. And the funerals and sepulchers of the dead shall not be disturbed in any way or upon any account.

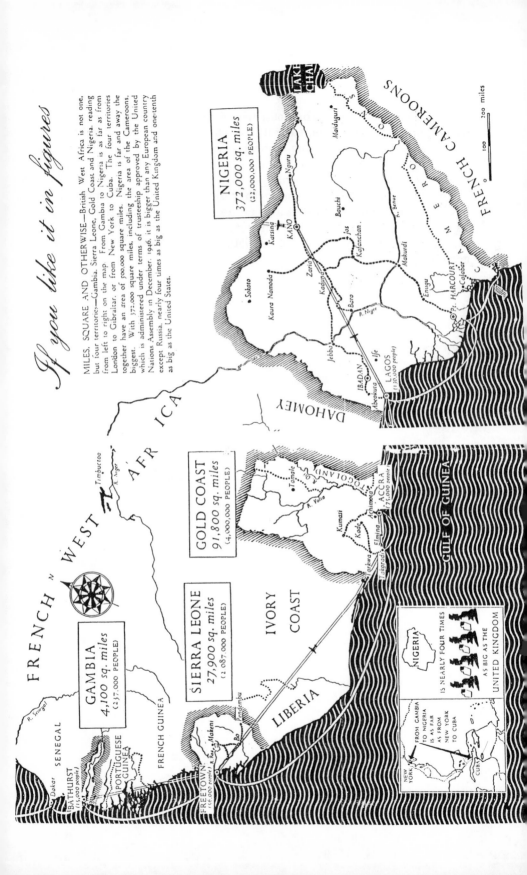

If you like it in figures

MILES, SQUARE AND OTHERWISE—British West Africa is not one, but four territories—Gambia, Sierra Leone, Gold Coast and Nigeria, reading from left to right on the map. From Gambia to Nigeria is as far as from London to Gibraltar, or from New York to Cuba. The four territories together have an area of 500,000 square miles. Nigeria is far and away the biggest. With 372,000 square miles, including the area of the Cameroons, which is administered under terms of trusteeship approved by the United Nations Assembly in December 1946, it is bigger than any European country except Russia, nearly four times as big as the United Kingdom and one-tenth as big as the United States.

FRENCH N WEST AFRICA

Timbuctoo

R. Niger

R. Senegal

Dakar

SENEGAL

BATHURST
(15,000 people)

GAMBIA
4,100 sq. miles
(237,000 PEOPLE)

PORTUGUESE GUINEA

FRENCH GUINEA

SIERRA LEONE
27,900 sq. miles
(2,087,000 PEOPLE)

Makeni
Bo
Pendembu
R. Rokel

FREETOWN
(60,000 people)

LIBERIA

IVORY
COAST

GOLD COAST
91,800 sq. miles
(4,000,000 PEOPLE)

Tamale
R. Volta
R. Volta
TOGOLAND
Kumasi
Kade
Achimota
Elmina
ACCRA
(75,000 people)
Takoradi
Sekondi

GULF OF GUINEA

NIGERIA
IS NEARLY FOUR TIMES
AS BIG AS THE
UNITED KINGDOM

FROM GAMBIA
TO NIGERIA
IS AS FAR
AS FROM
NEW YORK
TO CUBA
NEW YORK
CUBA

DAHOMEY

NIGERIA
372,000 sq. miles
(22,000,000 PEOPLE)

LAKE CHAD

Maiduguri

Nguru

Katsina

KANO

Sokato

Kaura Namoda

Zaria

Kadjina

Baro

Bauchi

Jos

Kajanchan

Makurdi

R. Benue

R. Niger

Jebba

IBADAN

Abeokuta

LAGOS
(130,000 people)

Ijfe

Enugu

Pt. HARCOURT

Calabar

FRENCH CAMEROONS

100   200 miles

A WHOLE SCENE GOING
OGUN AHOYAYA 1852
(The Boiling Battle of 1852)

CHAPTER 1
SUB-CHAPTER 1:1

OLUWOLE •
KOSOKO •
AKINTOYE •
COLONIAL GOVERNMENT •

The Boiling Battle of 1852 was significant in the history of juju music. It was this battle that brought the British to Lagos and the subsequent treaty of 1852 that abolished slavery.

The British brought colonial government to Lagos after the treaty was made and the colonial government brought the missionaries. The missionaries brought among other things the religion of Christianity. The religion of Christianity was accompanied by music played with tambourine and some other musical instruments. Lagos minstrels started playing a new type of music with the tambourine and this music was later named juju.

King Akintoye of Lagos (Reigned from 1841-1853)

Oba Akintoye I in the fight against his uncle Prince Kosoko for the obaship of Lagos, inadvertently brought juju music to Nigeria.

Prince Kosoko, heir-apparent to the throne of Lagos between 1834-1872 had twice been denied the throne. Chief Eletu Odibo, head of the kingmakers whom the prince claimed caused the premature demise of his mother by drowning, according to the prince was behind his denial of the throne. When the prince's auntie Madam Opo Olu, an exceptionally rich woman in control of over 1,400 slaves was accused of usury and witchcraft and banished from Lagos by King Oluwole whom the prince called an usurper, that was the last straw and the prince took to arms. The superior fire-power of the king's infantry was too overwhelming for Kosoko and he and his men were about to be captured when he fled to the neighboring Whydeh, taking with him the wife of Chief Eletu Odibo and at least scoring one on his arch-enemy. Once, Kosoko's men regrouped and made an invasion but all they did was looted the king's properties before they were sent back running.

King Oluwole reigned for six years (from 1834-1841) after his enthronement and in 1841, he died. When Oluwole died, a genuine effort was made this time to crown Kosoko the king but he was nowhere to be found at his place of exile. This was double luck for Chief Eletu Odibo who never really wanted him around in Lagos and he quickly installed the prince's nephew Akintoye the king. Akintoye, who knew that his acceptance of the throne would cause another war requested his uncle to come home and to join him in ruling Lagos. Chief Eletu Odibo warned him that firstly, it was not practical to have two reigning monarchies during the same period and secondly, all Kosoko would bring were problems; but the young king ignored the advice of the elders and consequently Kosoko came home.

Akintoye gave him a title and a palace and created a special court for him to live like royalty. His popularity started to soar. A very displeased Chief Eletu Odibo wanted none of these and out of sheer anger and frustration left Lagos in voluntary exile to Badagry. The departure of his great friend and advisor created unhappiness for the king and he demanded that the chief come home. Now Kosoko didn't want that; he rather would have the head of the kingmakers stay permanently in his self exile in Badagry. When the king insisted on his demand, Kosoko threatened to take the throne from him.

Chief Eletu Odibo was on his way back home on a boat with an army of Egbaland people when he was met with a barrage of gunfire by Kosoko's men on the Five Cowrie Creek. The gunfight that ensued didn't stop the chief from landing at the king's palace where he was welcomed home and embraced by his friend and king who was happy to see him back. The happy reunion of the king

Five Cowrie Creek

Landuji Tapa Oshodi

and the chief infuriated the prince. He attacked the king and involved him in the war. Interestingly enough, he simultaneously took on two armies—both the king's and the chief's— and he was winning. This time, luck was on his side. As the war dragged on, thirst became a problem for the chief's men. They were dying of thirst because the wells were all dried up and they had to turn to the salty river water to sustain themselves. This was why this war was called Ogun Olomiro—"The Battle of Salt Water" of June 1845.

Akintoye's men were losing the war as fast as they were recuperating so he was advised to go into exile but hotly in pursuit by Oshodi one of Kosoko's war leaders who was asked to bring his head back on the orders of Kosoko. At Agboyi Creek, Oshodi caught up with the fleeing king and captured him but for some strange reasons allowed him to go free. On the other side of the battle, Chief Eletu Odibo had been captured and Kosoko had ordered that he be drowned exactly in the same River McEwen (Mekune) were he claimed the chief drowned his mother. After three days of fierce battle Kosoko won and finally became the king of Lagos.

River Mekune

The return of Oshodi was not accompanied by Akintoye's head so with Akintoye still alive, Kosoko felt unsafe on the throne.

Bisiriyu Majolagbe Ashogbon (Chief Ashogbon of Lagos), the son of Akintoye's war chief (1849-1935). Died on December 5, 1935, aged 87 years.

Meanwhile, Akintoye had reached Badagry where he received some help and then went on to Fernando Po where he met with Consul John Beecroft, who at that time was the British Consul for the Bights of Benin and Biafra. He sought for the assistance of the British to regain his throne and the Consul obliged. With a detachment of British troops led by Commodore Henry William Bruce, Akintoye was back in Lagos to face Kosoko. With superior war materiel including cannons, fighting again began in earnest. The shell fire and the noise of the cannons that claimed victims in immense quantity, were just too overwhelming a first time experience for the Lagosians and this was the reason why they called the war the Boiling Battle which in Yoruba means Ogun Ahoyaya.

On January 1853, Akintoye regained the throne of Lagos. He signed a treaty with the British to abolish slavery and human sacrifice and to encourage the spreading of missionaries' work. Eight months after he signed the treaty on September 1853, he died.

Forty-seven years later after the missionaries had started their works and firmly entrenched their presence in Lagos, the Lagos minstrels started using some of the musical instruments that the missionaries were using to conduct their mass, all to the minstrels' advantage. The actual one that they started off with was the tambourine. Juju music was born out of it.

Meanwhile, in 1853, Dosunmu succeeded his father Akintoye without any problems and peace reigned.

Now, whatever happened to Kosoko and his henchmen? Well, when King Akintoye regained his throne in 1853, the first thing he did was repaid the debt of gratitude he owed to Kosoko's war chief, Oshodi by granting him amnesty. (*When Akintoye was losing the battle and fled, Kosoko asked Tapa Oshodi to pursue him and to bring his head back for him (Kosoko). At Agboyi Creek on his way to his mother's town at Abeokuta, Oshodi caught up and captured the fleeing ex-king but for some strange reasons, released him and allowed him to escape unharmed).* Oshodi refused the amnesty unless this was also extended to Kosoko. But this time, the King had learnt his lesson. He spurned Oshodi's demand and so Oshodi did not come home.

By now, Kosoko has learnt that the British who aided Akintoye in getting rid of him from Lagos were now in Lagos to stay and having tasted their fire-power, he was in no mood to tamper with them anymore. Moreover, in the nine article treaty that the British signed with the King after the war, article number nine had involved in the whole sordid affair, another super-power, the French, who were interested in the going-ons. So, Kosoko knew that if he ever contemplated emulating the method that Akintoye

Bight of Benin

Beecroft Street, named after Consul John Beecroft, the British Consul for the Bights of Benin and Biafra, who helped Akintoye to regain the throne of Lagos.

used, by he too going to the French and seeking their assistance in order to come back to Lagos, he would be turned down. The French were in collusion with the British, the British were ally of Akintoye and Akintoye was indirectly friendly with the French. It was as that copper-tight and as that simple. By 1853, Kosoko was now totally homesick and war weary. He sent feelers home to the reigning monarch, Dosunmu, who decided to make peace with him. With the approval of Consul Campbell, he was allowed to come back home with his men on some conditions: 1) that he renounced all hostilities of any kind whatsoever, and 2) that he renounced the claims he had on the ports of Palma and Lekki with all to be given back to the Lagos government. He did and he was allowed to come back home. He died on April 16, 1872. What about his war-men? Whatever became of them? Nothing of much significance was known about five of his war captains after their arrival back in Lagos from Epe with their beloved leader, Prince Kosoko. Ojo Adubiaro, Dada Anthonio, Oso Akanbi, Ajeniya and Posu all lived a quiet life and slipped into oblivion except the war general Landuji Tapa Oshodi. Oshodi was not a Yoruba and never an Idejo (Lagos landowner). He was from the Nupe tribe in the Northern region of Nigeria. When he settled in Lagos, he became a domestic of King Oshinlokun the father of Prince Kosoko and cast his lot with King Idewu Ojulari, Kosoko's brother who ascended to the throne of Lagos after the death of King Oshinlokun. During the power struggle between the two brothers, it was there he proved himself a superb military man and later fought on the side of Kosoko both at the battles of Salt Water of 1845 and the Boiling Battle of 1852. On his arrival back in Lagos, he lived in Epetedo, a downtown neighborhood of Lagos for six years where Oshodi Street was named after him. He worked very closely with the Lagos government and became a close friend of the then Governor of Lagos, John Hawley Glover, who gave him a sword in appreciation of the services he rendered to the government. He died on July 2, 1868.

Chief Ashogbon, Akintoye's war chief, the Chief Ashogbon of Lagos also had Ashogbon Street named after him at the mid-town Apogbon neighborhood of Lagos. He died some years after the war was over.

Eleven years before Kosoko's death in 1861, King Dosunmu ceded Lagos to the British. A big mistake! The treaty for the cession contained three articles. Article one gave away the rights of Nigerians to their natural resources. Article two disallowed the Nigerian kings to be called kings because, according to the British, only the king of England should be known and called king.

Iga Idunganran *(The modern Lagos King's palace)*

Cannons used in Ogun Ahoyaya of 1852, now decorate the frontage of the old
Iga Idungaran.

However, Oba which is the African signification of king was allowed to be used to identify the Lagos's king. Article three removed the claims of Lagosians and in effect Nigerians on their landed properties and made their Obas salaried.

King Dosunmu of Lagos who ceded Lagos to the British Government on the 6th day of August, 1861 (*Died 26th February, 1885*).

The following are the three Articles in the Treaty with Lagos, in 1861:

Treaty With Lagos, 1861

Treaty between Norman B. Bedingfield, Commander of Her Majesty's Ship "PROMETHEUS" and Senior officer of the Bights Division, and William McCorskry, Esquire, Her Brittanic Majesty's Acting Consul, on the part of her Majesty the Queen of Great Britain and Docemo, Oba of Lagos on the part of himself and chiefs.

Article I

In order that the Queen of England may be the better enabled to assist, defend and protect the inhabitants of Lagos, and to put an end to Slave Trade in this land and the neighboring countries and to prevent the destructive wars so frequently undertaken by Dahomey and others for the Capture of Slaves, I, Docemo, do with the consent and advice of my Council, give, transfer and by this presents grants and confirm into the Queen of Great Britain, her heirs, and successors for ever, the port and Island of Lagos, with all the rights, profits, territories and appurtenances and whatsoever, thereto belonging and as well the profits and revenue as the direct, full and absolute dominion and sovereignty of the said port, island and premises, with all the royalties thereof, freely, fully, entirely and absolutely.

I do also covenant and grant that the quiet and peaceable possession thereof shall, with all possible speed, be freely and effectually delivered to the Queen of Great Britain or such person as her Majesty shall thereunto appoint for her use in the performance of this grant, the inhabitants of the said island and territories, as the Queen's subjects, and under her sovereignty, crown jurisdiction, and government, being still suffered to live there.

Article II

Decemo will be allowed the use of the title King in its usual African signification (Oba), and will be permitted to decide disputes between natives of Lagos with their consent, subject to appeal to the British laws.

Article III

In the transfer of funds, the stamp of Docemo affixed to the document will be proof that there are no other native claims upon it, and for this purpose he will be permitted to use it as hitherto.

In consideration of the cession as before-mentioned of the port and island and territories of Lagos, the representatives of the Queen of Great Britain do promise, subject to the approval of Her Majesty, that Docemo shall receive an annual pension from the Queen of Great Britain equal to the revenue hitherto annually received by him; such pension to be paid at such periods and in such mode as may hereafter be determined.

Lagos, August 6, 1861.

Following are dates of noted important events during this period.

1. On 1st January, 1852, Queen Victoria of England presented to King Akintoye of Lagos, a silver mounted staff.

2. On 2nd September, 1853, King Akintoye of Lagos died.

3. On 3rd September, 1853, Dosunmu, Akintoye's eldest son became the king of Lagos.

4. On 6th June, 1859, the CMS Grammar School was founded.

5. On Friday 22nd June, 1860, The "Anglo African" was the first newspaper ever to be published in Lagos by Robert Campbell.

6. On 6th August, 1861, Lagos was ceded to the British Crown.

7. On 30th March, 1867, foundation stone of Christ Church, Lagos was laid by Governor John Hawley Glover.

8. On 19th May, 1873, Ejinrin market was opened for trade.

9. On April, 1878, the Wesleyan (later Methodist) Boys' High School was opened in Lagos and Rev. W.B. Euba (an African) was made the Principal of the school from 1889-1896.

10. On 11th May, 1878, the Lagos Faji Market was opened for trade and marketing.

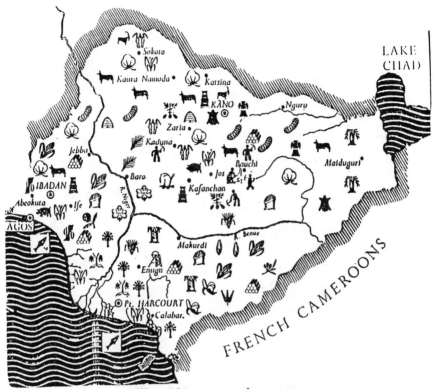

West African natural resources

On August 6, 1891, Oba Dosunmu (Docemo) ceded Lagos to the British in a treaty containing 8 articles. The very first article of the total eight was the one that gave away the rights of the country's natural resources (above) to the British. Similar deals were also cut with three other West African countries viz. Gold Coast (Ghana), Sierra Leone, and Gambia, releasing the rights of their natural resources (below) to the British.

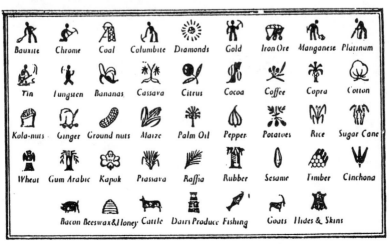

West African Editors visiting Bournville Chocolate factory.

Prince Aminu Kosoko--Great grandson of Prince Kosoko of Lagos

Chief Bajulaiye Jiyabi II, present Chief Eletu Odibo of Lagos, is seen pointing to a split in the mystery tree at the Isale Eko neighborhood of Lagos.

11. On 28th February, 1889, the foundation stone of St. John's Church (Aroloya) was laid by Mr. John Otunba Payne.

12. On 29th June, 1880, St. Paul's Church (Breadfruit) was opened for service.

13. On 26th February, 1885, King Dosunmu of Lagos died.

2

THE MISSIONARIES

MISSIONARY WORK •
MARY SLESSOR •
THOMAS BIRCH FREEMAN •
CHRISTIANITY •

T he colonial government paved the way for the arrival of missionaries in Lagos but since the days of the early Portuguese explorers and traders, West Africa had attracted the attention of missionary societies. A group called the Catholic Fathers in the early sixteenth century was the first known missionaries in Benin in Nigeria. It was years later that other missionaries followed suit. Behind trade and acquisition of colonies, missionary work was one of the great western civilizing influences on West Africa. By the nineteenth century, mission work had firmly established itself on the coast and grown with early starters like Renner and Hartwig of the Church Missionary Society who settled in Sierra Leone in April 1804. Thirty-one years later in Gold Coast (Ghana) it was the Methodists. Their first successful attempt was in 1835 by the

Wesleyan Missionary Society. In Gambia and the Cameroons, other missionary societies of different denominations followed.

Later in the century, the White Fathers of Algiers crossed the Sahara to establish a center in Navrongo in the Northern Territories of the Gold Coast. First of the inland salvo.

Mary Slessor

When missionary work first started, the missionaries sometimes without the help of the government took their task under great adversity to places where dangers were omnipresent. Some died, some survived but they were never deterred. Immediately one crumbled, another was at the ready for replacement.

Two of the most heroic were Mary Slessor and Thomas Birch Freeman. Mary Slessor was from Dundee in Scotland in Great Britain. She lived alone for over twenty years in a wild stretch of country near the Cross River in Nigeria. By her force of character, she won the devotion of the indigenes of Eastern Nigeria until her name became synonymous with anything that was right and progressive in the district. She died in the old Eastern Nigeria.

Thomas Birch Freeman

Thomas Birch Freeman was a missionary in the Gold Coast. Recorded in his diary were times when the African drumbeats of the natives was a sign that human sacrifice by the king was in

Christ Church Cathedral, Lagos

Salvation Army, Lagos

progress and which he sought to stop. With the missionaries came not only the teachings of Christianity but also modern ideas on health and sanitation. They built schools, hospitals and leper settlements.

Today, churches, cathedrals and chapels that are seen in many African cities; elementary, high and trade schools; colleges and universities in country after country; dispensaries, maternity homes, leper settlements and hospitals, are all evidences of the solid foundation work in spiritual, educational and medical side of the missionaries carried on by their trainees that passed them down from generation to generation.

Possibly these were the reasons why, when the colonial government started having problems with the new generation of natives that had received proper education and were brilliant and audacious enough to question and challenge the "fine prints" in the treaties signed with their forefathers, the missionaries became a separate entity from the white rulers, but loved and unmolested.

St. Peters Church, Lagos

Mary Slessor grave in the old Eastern Nigeria

3

"JUJU"

*FIRST THEORY OF HOW JUJU
MUSIC OBTAINED ITS NAME*

SUPERSTITION •
HERBALISM •
EXTRA SENSORY PERCEPTION (ESP) •

*Take the Efinrin grass leaves, the bark of the sour-plum tree and
the pako roots. Put them all in an earthenpot. Add water and boil.
Take a cupful of the potion and your stomach-ache is gone.
Better still, take the claw of an eagle, the tail of a lizard, the head of
a serpent and the horn of a ewe. Tie all together in a bunch, place
beneath the nose and inhale deeply and your head-ache is gone.
And that's not all; escape dramatically from a nasty accident with
an African charm hanging around your neck and you're on the
side of the gods.*

These are ju-ju the satirical terms that the Christian converts
applied to African religion of idolatry and herbalism that were practiced before recorded history. From time immemorial, herbalism, incan-

tations, sacrifice, etc., were orders of the day in African society. Native therapeutics and prophylaxis could not be separated from spiritualism; they were all interwoven. They were rooted in tradition and the tradition lived in the medicine-man.

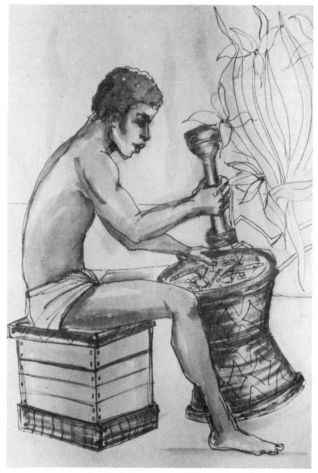

The medicine-man at work
"...the medicine-man will still mix a potion, make a charm or propitiate the gods at times of alarm and disaster and the potions, at least, are often extremely efficacious

When the missionaries came and brought the western religion of Christianity to Lagos, in practical known facts, they never forced the Lagosians to convert. Acceptance of it was voluntary. The realization of the missionaries that the medicine-man will still mix a potion, make a charm or propitiate the gods at times of alarm and disaster—and the potions, at least, are often extremely efficacious made them to be very careful about condemning what they didn't know anything about and left alone the part that the medicine-man could still play in the African society.

The problem was the Lagosians themselves because anytime that there was an instance in which the native medicine did not perform in the way it claimed should, the converts were always quick to point at its uselessness. Till these days, they still have not let up. A case in point was a building collapse disaster of the late 1950s in Lagos.

Mount Carmel School on the mainland of Lagos was a girls' Catholic mission school that pride itself in training young Nigerian girls in basic high school education plus commercial courses like typing, short-hand, bookkeeping, accounting, commerce and trade. Its popularity was attracting girls in large numbers and because of overflow, it decided to expand by building an annex. Construction of the annex was given to a native contractor who employed construction workers to put up the building. Everything had gone very well and the building was half way completed when one day without any warning, tragedy struck. On the morning of that day, the workers arrived at work in good mood and nothing was in the air to suggest an impending danger. None of the workers arrived at work complaining about the usual African bad omen of stubbing his left big toe on a stump or having a black bird flying over his head and striking his face with its wing etc, etc. They all started their work with their usual jollity. But just before noon time, without any warning, the building crashed, and buried the workers in the rubbles. Like lightning, news of the catastrophe spread and the Lagos Fire Brigade, Boys Scouts and rescuers of all kinds converged on the school to ferret out the survivors. Miraculously there were two dead. The rest of the construction workers were all wounded and they were taken to the hospital for treatment. One of the two dead was the head of the construction workers and he was not accounted for until days later. Now comes the point: Why was he not found earlier? There is a charm in the Nigerian circle of native medicine known as "egbe" meaning 'shift'. This charm could be in form of a pendant hanging around one's neck or as a ring located on one's finger or toe etc, etc. Its performance is specific. At the instance of an occurrence that constitute danger, its magical powers shifts the wearer or the charm possessor from the scene of the occurrence to safety. Miners wear it, so do divers, construction workers, sailors and people whose works go hand in hand with danger.

Now, the head of the construction workers of the Mount Carmel School building was usually seen wearing the charm around his neck and when he could not be accounted for earlier on, it was concluded that the "shift" charm had shifted him away from the accident to a safe place and he would resurface later.

In the initial stage of the time of his disappearance, juju medicine men came out of their revered places extolling the efficacy of native medicine but when in the days following there was no reappearance of the gentleman, soft talk tempered by moderacy started to prevail. After three days, soft wind blowing over the disaster area started to carry a putrid smell that was offensive to passers-by in the area and who happened to smell a whiff of the stench. Rescuers were alerted to the smell which was traced to a particular point under the debris. When the bricks and metals were removed, there, was the grisly, rotten, smashed-to-pulp by the debris, body of the unfortunate leader. It was a piteous spectacle.

Now, incident such as this were the ones that converts usually use to feel justified about their charge that there was nothing to native medicine but vileness and ignorance.

But two points of argument always work well in favor of native medicine. First one is, before the arrival of Christianity that brought western health program, the parents and grandparents of the converts had always relied on native medicine fo their health and survival and it was into native medicine that they, the converts, were born and brought up. Second one is, just exactly as native medicine fails to work successfully on occasions, western medicine also fails and at times with disastrous results. Not all head-ache tablets cure head-aches and thalidomide tablets would not have caused the birth of limbless and retarded children if they did the work that they were supposed to do, to give just two examples. Besides, organic medicine, the basis of western medicine, is derived from nature just exactly as herbalism the basis of native medicine does.

The strong belief that a lot of people have in "shift" is solidly reflected in the record that composer and agidigbo music exponent Adeolu Akinsanya made in memory of the disaster. It goes thus:

> To eat and to drink is an important matter
> And this is what brought the builders to the Catholic
> The person who does not work has lost his right to eat
> And this is what brought the builders to the Catholic
> Building collapsed, building collapsed, and here we go again
> And to earth, two people returneth.
> Man proposes but God disposes.

If the builders had known that the building would collapse
They wouldn't have gone to work on that day.
But suddenly the building collapsed.
Dust scattered.
Melee ensued.
News reverberated through the neighborhoods.
The head builder was the one I felt sorry for most
For good three days, he was under the rubbles.
Everybody was searching for him
But couldn't find him
Nobody slept
Nobody rested
Could he have run away?
Could he have flown away?
Could "shift" have shifted him (to safety)?
But lo!, he was under the rubbles.

Interestingly enough, many African countries, nowadays in the 21st century, are now paying more heed to and giving accreditation to native medicine resulting in many European countries sending personnels of their health establishments to learn and make research into the native medicine in these African countries.

Native medicine also known as herbalism, idolatry somehow referred to as paganism and ESP the acronym for Extra Sensory Perception, all interwove to make the religion that the Yoruba founders of Lagos practiced and which was derisively and variously called ogun, juju, voodoo, witchcraft and bad magic.

This religion has a light and a dark side to it. The light side which is basically healing of ailments when successful, hardly make a whisper. The dark side roars its presence when it arrives in the limelight.

To listen to the old king of juju music, Tunde King, tell of his experiences with the dark side of native medicine in connection with the music during his hay days is to understand why the Christian and muslim converts were implored not to even insinuate that idolatry, herbalism, or the native religion in general were nothing but vileness and ignorance.

According to him, Tunde King was billed to play at a certain social occasion with a good and upcoming juju group of which leader was Ojoge Daniel. Along the way in his musical career, Tunde had built a large fan and it did not occur to him that that was the day he was going to taste a full blast effect of "juju" (voodoo, native medicine) the satirical term that had been applied to his music by the converts, all because of jealousy. Ojoge Daniel took

the stage first and when it was over with him, he, Tunde was ready
to perform. As he and his boys picked up their instruments and
tested then, not a sound came out of them. The microphones were
all dead and electricity from particular outlets where plugs were to
be inserted, had seized to be flowing. Minutes before this incident,
a Tunde's fan had noticed a suspicious looking character standing
by where Tunde's musical instruments were packed; and he had
apparently been also noticed reciting incantations. Then, this die-
hard fan of Tunde went and brought a gravel, placed it on the
instruments and started to recite his own incantations. In time, the
numbness were unlocked, the electricity returned and sound came
back to the microphones and the musical instruments. Tunde then
was able to perform. Tunde did not blame this on Ojoge Daniel but
on the fans of their idol who liked to foment trouble. He concluded
that, that was the way Akanbi Ege died; that he was poisoned. But
Akanbi Ege's death was a slightly different story even though it
was connected with "juju". The gentleman was a brilliant mind
as far as juju music was concerned and was rapidly climbing to
the top when he committed a cardinal sin. In Nigeria where a little
disagreement over political views could draw blood and death, it
was always fatal when music players mixed music with politics.
Akanbi Ege was of Saro extraction. He had dropped his last
english name of Wright (Akanbi Wright) and had cast his lot with
the Yoruba-Saro dominated political party NNDP (Nigeria
National Democratic Party) of the 1923 founded by the great Herbert
Macaulay. Before Macaulay's death in 1946, the NCNC (National
Council of Nigeria and the Cameroons) was formed (Macaulay
was the first President of the NCNC) and the NNDP had allied
itself with it. The NCNC was also known as the "Demo," short for
democratic. Most of the elements of this party were of the Ibo tribal
people and this made politics seemed to be based on tribalism. The
Yorubas under the leadership of Chief (the Chief came later)
Obafemi Awolowo then formed a cultural group called Egbe Omo
Oduduwa after the formation of the NCNC. This group was later
turned into a political party known as the Action Group in the 1950s,
in opposition to the NCNC, the "Demo." The AG (Action Group)
controlled the Western Region of Nigeria, homeland of the
Yorubas. Needing more base to operate, the AG rightly or wrongly
theorized that Lagos, the capital of Nigeria, founded by the Yorubas,
belonged to the Western Region of Nigeria. This brought a sharp
conflict between the NCNC and the AG.

  Now, Akanbi Ege then went and made a record called *Demo lo
l'Eko* (Demo is the owner of Lagos) supporting the NCNC in its
fierce opposition of allowing Lagos to be merged with the West.

This record became a hit and it irritated a lot of the Yorubas in Lagos and in their homeland of the West. He probably did himself in with this record because subsequently, he mysteriously became crippled, suffered for a long time with this crippling ailment before he eventually died. It was believed that "juju" was cast on him to punish him for that record and for his support of the NCNC because he was a Yoruba who turned his back against his people.

In conclusion, the Christian converts found affluence in Christianity, in the place of worship, in the western dress and the music that Christianity employed in conducting mass. When the Lagos minstrels started using the tambourine to accompany their songs, the converts reacted unfavorably to this. They could not bear to see one of the musical instruments that they use for their worship in the hands of street entertainers. They regarded it as sacrilegious. But there was nothing they could do about it because the minstrels were not breaking the law. Satirizing the music with a derogatory name of juju (which they now gave to their original religion) was their only way of showing contempt for the minstrel's music. But this is a theory that never went down too well because many years later, juju music obtained its name from a more plausible source.

HISTORY OF JUJU MUSIC

4

1900-1910

CHRISTIANS •
MINSTRELSY •
TAMBOURINE •
THE EARLY JUJU •

By 1900, Nigeria had long been defined. Lagos was its "eye" and it was teeming with activities. Fourteen years later in 1914, it was made its capital. The population kept soaring. Some freed slaves from Freetown, who were resettled in Sierra Leone by British philanthropists that formed the Sierra Leone Company, decided to come back home to Lagos. They regrouped and congregated in some certain neighborhoods. Now known or variously called "Saro," the returnees or repatriates, they added to the population and made Lagos more colorful. As a port city, sailors and crewmen could be seen everywhere. Bars, cafes and hotels were always filled with clientels. In the day time minstrels could be seen everywhere. Nightfall also always brought out many different entertaining characters. Within four decades, the colonial government had changed Lagos considerably. Its so called "beautiful period" was at times punctuated by some few ugliness which in the sum total added color to the atmosphere. Lagos had its share of underworld characters that occasionally made headlines and brought in diverting excitements. Among these characters were *Ojiji Logbologbo, Ogogoluoluo, Orehin Gbakumo,* and *Akintoye Baba,* the "Ebute-Elefun assassin."

Of all the underworld denizens, Akintoye was the mythical. He engaged in burglary in broad daylight knowing fully well that he could not be caught. All he had to do was lie on his back and he became invisible. Myth had it that a ring located on the big toe of his right foot caused his invisibility. After attempts to catch him had proved fruitless, he usually rose and walked away when the police and everybody had gone and the dust had cleared. Lagosians loved to talk about Akintoye. His disappearing act gave them more excitement than his burglarious activities.

When talk was not centered around Akintoye and the rest of the underworld figures, other targets were usually the obaship of Lagos, the colonial government and politics.

By 1910, a new crop of Lagosians that had received the western education brought by the missionaries had seen through the evil of the treaty and had started creating problems for the colonial government. The reigning oba at this time was Oba Esugbayi Eleko I, a very controversial figure (*see The ELEKO AFFAIR in A WHOLE SCENE GOING Page 44*).

Christianity had brought affluence. Its music had started to turn daily life around. First were the minstrels who had started to use tambourine and also the samba drum, instruments that were popular with Christian religious groups. Reaction by the Christian converts to the minstrels using the instruments that they (the Christians) used to conduct their mass, was sharp and uncompromising. They regarded it as sacrilegious. But there was very little they could do about it because Article 8 of the treaty that abolished slavery embraced freedom of whatever anyone wanted to do within the confines of law. The minstrels were not breaking the law and satire was the only thing left for the converts to resort to. And so they did.

The very converts that had turned their backs to paganism and had called herbalism, incantations and extrasensory perceptions, juju, their term for vileness, now satirically applied the word to the new music. But this is a theory that did not hold much ground in the naming of juju music. Years to come, the music got its name from a more plausible account.

However, among much more early famous minstrels was the tall, good looking, sweet voiced, lovable Awerende Elemuayo; an ever

OREHIN GBAKUMO

OGOGO LUOLUO

OJIJI LOGBOLOGBO

AKINTOYE BABA The Ebutte-Elefun assasin

Underworld denizens

smiling harmless entertaining character. Balancing a gourd of palm-wine on his head, he went about the streets singing, combining

Awerende Elemu-ayo

selling with minstrelsy. In addition to selling palm-wine, he also danced and sang and one could not help giving him more money for his additional efforts. His famous song which always brought people out of their houses was:

> *N ole fija sewo o; n ole fija sewo o*
> *Awerende Elemuayo; n ole fija sewo o;*
>   *which means:*
> *I cannot start the day with argument*

> *I cannot start the day with argument*
> *Here comes Awerende, seller of unadulterated*
>   *palm-wine*
> *I cannot start the day with argument.*

He never wanted bargaining. In one minute there went a minstrel, in another, a troubadour and that was Lagos. There were many types of music going on and the city was fun.

WHAT KIND OF MUSIC
WAS JUJU MUSIC?

The playing of juju music started off with a lone man and his lone drum (usually the tambourine or the framed rectangular samba drum) going about the streets singing, accompanied by this drum. His music originally had no name to it. Referred to popularly as a minstrel, he usually held a low wage job in the day time. To supplement his low earning and be able to live fairly comfortably but most possibly for love of music, he played in the night in the streets, going door to door.

Who were his clients? This music maker knew the residences of the rich and the famous and as he went about the streets playing, he usually stopped at their gates or doors to play. On most of his lucky days when these city elites were at home enjoying their leisure time in their parlours or at their windows enjoying public scenes, he was always noticed. This was a guarantee of good gift in form of cash money.

What type of songs did he sing or play? Name praising songs primarily. Secondarily, songs about current events in the country and morality songs also.

How did he play his music? He always started off with singing quickly followed by the drum to accompany the song. Holding the drum usually on his left hand, the fingers and palm of the right hand were always used to hit, tap or knock the membranous musical instrument held on the left hand. The drum supplied rhythm to his melodious song.

After playing for a while, he sometimes stopped, played a drum solo, then returned with the song to end up the number.

The music was usually the solemn four beats to a bar 4/4 and in rear cases the faster 4/8 or 4/16 type. The voice was usually good-singing nature-gifted or the unique type associated with the minstrel. Outwardly his nature was the good demeanor type because if he failed to win a cash gift after playing, he moved on showing no animosity towards his tight-fisted client.

What kind of a person was he? An intelligent person who kept abreast of what was going on, who philosophized and who tipped off clients about an impending danger. The lack of means to be institutionally educated was made up for the cleverness he showed in his self-employed part-time job. Some rich and famous, moved by the name praising songs, usually gave him substantial cash gift to show appreciation. Through his songs, he had the power to change mood or cause emotion to be displayed by memorializing an event with a good or emotional song.

Music makers of this kind were all over Lagos around the 1920s. Soon, social demands started to change things around for them.
What were social demands? Social occasions that called for merrymaking like weddings, birthday parties, house warming parties, graduation day ceremonies, street festivals etc., which demanded a group of musicians to liven up the place and create jollity by making invitees to dance and enjoy themselves.

Because of social demands, some minstrels found themselves forming groups. Stores in Lagos were now stocking string instruments like guitars, banjos, mandolines, ukuleles, banjo-mandolines, ukulele-guitars, etc., and minstrels now started playing string instruments also. A four member juju group was soon established. This was in the mid 1930s and it was in this particular decade that the music became known as juju. Instrumentations of juju music were one string instrument, the tambourine, sekere, (the gourd rattle) and a supporting vocalist.
Songs of juju groups did not change from where they drew their origin. They were still name praising, current events, morality, philosophy and also prayers. These were what their clients wanted and this was why they endured. As for the rhythm, this changed drastically because with three more men, the percussion became much more full bodied. Singing became much more communal and different styles developed.

The call and response style in which the lead vocal, usually the leader, called and of which response from the rest of the players came back, was one of the new styles. Harmony was another new style. The beat could be fast, medium or slow in tempo. After engagement, distribution of money depended on hierarchy. The leader usually took the biggest share. The remainder was then junked in the trickle down process. But everybody was always happy.

As time passed, juju groups increased in size and the original four member group became history.

A WHOLE SCENE GOING
THE ELEKO AFFAIR

ELEKO •
NIGERIA'S FIRST POLITICAL PARTY •
HERBERT MACAULAY •
NNAMDI AZIKIWE •
OBAFEMI AWOLOWO •

At the time that the seed of juju music was germinating and right up to its radicle and subsequent shoot, the following were among things that were happening in Lagos in a whole scene going:

THE ELEKO AFFAIR (The Iju Waterworks)

In 1900, Oba Esugbayi Eleko, the grandson of the late Oba Dosunmu (who ceded Lagos to the British) ascended the throne of Lagos. Around this time, the colonial government proposed a plan that would bring water that ran through pipe tubings to Lagos. The cost of this pipe borne water scheme was around one hundred and thirty thousand pounds sterling (£130,000) and it was to be defrayed by the Lagosians through tax. Eleko objected! The government angrily reacted to Eleko's objection and charged that the plan was for the betterment of the health of the Lagosians. Eleko, whose objection had nothing to do with the plan but to the cost of the plan that the government had asked his subjects to bear, quickly shot back by saying that it was the white people who wanted water faucets and it was the white people who should pay the cost because as far as he was concerned, the Lagosians' old well water was good enough for them. Despite strong objections, at Iju, not far away from Lagos, the Waterworks was built. The levy became a very serious issue with the people of Lagos and eight years later, Eleko was forced to lead an anti-government protest march of about 15,000 Lagosians on Government House. During this march, the colonial rule for the first time was threatened because after shops and stores belonging to white people were looted and valuable properties stolen and damaged, there were followed riots and market strikes.

The Iju Waterworks building today

After all the improvements that it had brought to Lagos, the colonial government was stunned to see that Eleko's influence was much more ingrained in the people than its authority. At this particular year of 1908, something important happened. The first political party in Nigeria was formed. It was called People's Union. One of the founders, Dr. John Randle, a Yoruba, was its

Eshugbayi Eleko, Lagos most controversial king together with Dr. Herbert Macaulay, gave the British their toughest time in Nigeria.

Dr. John Randle, one of the founders of the first political party in Lagos – The Peoples Union. (*Died 27th of February, 1928*)

Dr. Orisadipe Obasa – First General Secretary of The Peoples
Union.

chairman and Dr. Orisadipe Obasa, another Yoruba, became the party's first secretary. Six years later in 1914, the Water-rate Affair similarly known as Eleko Affair, had split Lagos into pro and anti-government factions. The Peoples Union was initially anti-government in the affair but when it was threatened with sedition, it backed off and supported the government. With increased stipends as incentives to traditional rulers and legislative appointments to pro- government Lagos educated elites, the white rulers were able to sway a large number of Lagosians to their side. Then another important thing happened which was to shape the course of Nigeria's history. A Yoruba Lagosian gentleman by the name of Herbert Samuel Heelas Macaulay, a strong anti-imperialist who co-owned a daily publication *The Daily News*, with Dr. John Akinlade Caulcrick, another Yoruba, refused to be bought and supported Eleko to the hilt. Herbert Macaulay was influential. His father, the Rev. Thomas Babington Macaulay who hailed from Ore Aganju in the district of Ikirun, a province of Oyo, a heartland of the Yorubas, was founder and first principal of the Church Missionary Society (CMS) Grammar School, in Lagos (the CMS Grammar School is the oldest high school in Nigeria today). Ever since colonialism had reared its head in Nigeria, he had been a thorn in its flesh. He was exceptionally intelligent, fearless, volatile, fiercely and wholeheartedly nationalistic. He fervently believed that no white man on the face of the earth was superior to a black man; and that there was no heavenly or earthly reason for the white people to shape the destiny of the black people. Given time, he believed that all the so called improvements brought by the whites could be accomplished by blacks. Till his dying day he was constantly in western attire with his ever present bow-tie not only to ridicule the whites but to constantly remind them that they weren't superior. In Ilesha, he was nicknamed "Gbogungboro" (the warrior leader). In Lagos, his residence, in front of the rear-end of the general post-office at marina, was named Kirsten Hall, and he was known as "The Wizard of Kirsten". The people of Offa nicknamed him "Oyinbo alawo dudu" (the white man with a black skin) because of his intellect that was on par with the white rulers. The Lagosians called him "Ejo n'gboro" (snake in the city). This last nickname was probably the one that said a lot about him. The habitat of the serpent is the wild; but when it comes to the point where its presence is felt in the city, then city dwellers better start getting nervous. And that was exactly what Macaulay was to the white colonial government--a source of nervousness.

He supported the Eleko against the government in the WATER RATE LEVY. He supported the Eleko again in the CENTRAL

Herbert Macaulay's father, Rev. Thomas Babington Macaulay founder and the first Principal of the C.M.S. Grammar School, Lagos (founded 6th June, 1859). (Died in 1878)

Herbert Samuel Heelas Macaulay, CE (Founder of the National Democratic Party, 1923) "The Champion and Defender of Native Rights and Liberties (*1864-1946. Aged 82 years*).

MOSQUE APPOINTMENT AFFAIR where Eleko approved the
appointment and accepted the invitation of the Central Mosque for
the installation of Bashorun and other chiefs, a job and ceremony
the colonial government felt the Eleko should have stayed away
from. On this issue, Eleko's stipend was suspended and his
recognition as Oba was temporarily put on hold in 1919. He
represented Eleko with the Oba's famous staff in London in the famous OLUWA LANDCASE (See Oluwa Landcase in A WHOLE
SCENE GOING on page 49) where he made controversial statements
to the British press that Eleko, the Oba of Lagos was paid less than the
lowest paid European gardener in Lagos; that the pension of £300
annually promised Eleko's grandfather Dosunmu had never been
paid and that Eleko's palace had neither been improved nor
renovated in years. The colonial government was put on the spot on
this issue because the British government in Great Britain reacted
angrily to these embarrassing statements. Back at home, the
colonial government with Sir Hugh Clifford as the Governor and
Commander-in-Chief of Nigeria, was furious. It wanted Eleko to
denounce Macaulay. He refused. He was deposed and on August 6,
1925, banished and sent to Oyo. Eleko's case was taken to the Privy
Council, the highest court in Great Britain but two years later, in
1928, when the colonial government knew that it was going to lose
the case, decided to settle it out of court. Eleko did win the out-of-court
settlement and preparation for bringing him home from
banishment was under way when something happened. It was
Macaulay again.

Macaulay, in his newspaper, the Lagos Daily News, on June 29,
1925, published an article alleging that the colonial government
was planning to plant gunpowder in the vehicle that would bring
Eleko back home from Oyo so that it would explode and blow him to
pieces thereby putting an end to his life. The colonial government
reacted with rage. First, the (controversial) Water Rate Levy;
second, the (spiteful) Central Mosque Appointment Affair; third,
the Oluwa Land Case and the (inglorious) statement to the press in
London and now the (diabolical) GUNPOWDER PLOT allegation.
Well, that was it!. The colonial government had had enough of
Macaulay. He was arrested, charged, tried, and sent to prison on
Monday the 26th of August 1928. To show their intense dislike for
him, he was given six months imprisonment with hard labor and
without the option of a fine whereas Dr. John Akinlade Caulcrick,
co-owner of the newspaper was just fined fifty-pounds sterling
(£50) with the alternative of a three-month jail term. Whether the
gunpowder plot story was true or not, it certainly did one thing; it
assured the safe arrival of Eleko from Oyo because if in truth the

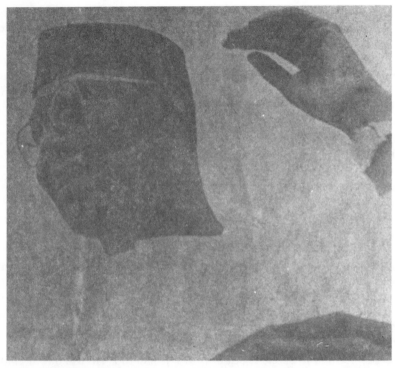

Dr. Nmamdi Azikiwe, first president of the Federal Republic of Nigeria and the alter ego of Chief Obafemi Awolowo.

Chief Obafemi Awolowo, leader of the Yoruba political party. A man of great vision and foresight.

colonial government had planned it, Macaulay's revelation had stopped it from being carried out. On July 4, 1931, Eleko returned to Lagos to a tumultuous hero's welcome. Markets, shops, offices were closed for an un-official holiday. It was crass folly on the part of the colonial government to have sent Macaulay to prison because what followed after his jail terms changed the course of history in Nigeria and ushered in a new era in Nigerian politics. On June 14, 1923, five years before he was sent to prison, Macaulay had formed a political party, The Nigerian National Democratic Party (NNDP). When he returned from prison, his anti-imperial activities became virulent. His political party became stronger. This time, he just didn't want people of the city of Lagos to cling to his coat-tail; he wanted the whole nation of Nigeria with its diverse tribal people to rally round him to fight the white people not only in Nigeria but in the whole of Africa.

Out of many Nigerians who later joined the NNDP was a Nigerian who was later to become a doctor of Literature and owner of a daily publication called the African Pilot. An Ibo by tribe, Dr. Nnamdi Azikiwe found his mentor in Herbert Macaulay. Dutifully, and conscientiously, he worked closer to the elder founder of the party like a son. Around the 1940s, a young Yoruba man by the name of Jeremiah Oyeniyi Obafemi Awolowo, freshly out of school, had just taken to journalism and found what was going on very exciting. Azikiwe had become Macaulay's megaphone and had started megaphoning the leader's anti-imperialist activities through series of lectures. Assigned to cover some of these lectures, Awolowo's mind was blown to bits by the sheer brilliance and dynamism of Azikiwe to the point of saying about the lecturer that here was a man academically competent and self-confident enough to run through the pages of all history. As for Herbert Macaulay, Awolowo truly believed that he was the champion and defender of native rights and liberty. But before he left Nigeria in the early 1940s to study law in Great Britain, he had started to have doubts about elements in the NNDP whose ideas he was espoused to. About this time, on May 7, 1946, Herbert Macaulay died. On the day he died, Lagos was grinded to a halt. His funeral was an event that the Lagosians had never seen its type before, and would never forget. The memory of it lived forever, particularly in children born in Lagos before World War II.

Dr. Herbert Macaulay, C.E. (in his last days). Variously known as Ejo N'gboro, Oyinbo alawo dudu, The Duke of Kirsten etc., etc., he set a lasting mark in Nigerian politics which to this day has not been suprassed, equalled or rivalled. A great man, a great Nigerian. A great African.

Young Azikiwe, eulogizing at Macaulay's funeral

A WHOLE SCENE GOING
THE OLUWA LANDCASE

Sir Hugh Clifford Governor of Lagos (1919-1925)

CHAPTER 5
SUB-CHAPTER 5:1

Herbert Macauley Esq. C.E.
Champion and defender of native rights and liberties

CHIEF AMODU TIJANI OLUWA •
HERBERT MACAULAY •
THE PRIVY COUNCIL •
"SEIGNEURIAL RIGHT" •

The Eleko Affair was intertwined with the Oluwa Landcase and the isolation of one to be treated separately and fully would simply result in the clamour to know exactly what the other one was simply all about too. To this end, here goes:

The Oluwa Landcase was one of the most racist and worst exhibition of arrogance of power by the Colonial Government that was administering its rule over Nigeria during the country's pre-independence days.

What was the Oluwa Landcase all about? It was an incredulous attempt by the white rulers to violate the principle of ownership in order to establish a system of placing native lands at the disposal and under the control of the white Governor of the land.

In the middle part of June 1912, a committee had sat down in the Colonial Office at Downing Street in London to consider the whole question of Land Legislation in the Northern provinces of Nigeria (a similar one was convened in the earlier part of June 1912 on other West African Dependences) and had concluded that all the Hausas' lands whether occupied or unoccupied shall be placed entirely under the control and subject to the disposition of the white Governor who shall hold and administer them for the use and common benefit of the Natives whose title to the occupation and the use of such native lands shall not be valid without the consent of the Governor! What does this mean in the layman terms? Simply, it means that to be able to use the land that one owned as a native (in one own's country), whether for real estate, farming or whatever, one had to get permission or go-ahead sign from the Governor who might refuse if he, the Governor, needed it for his whatever reasons. Sheepishly and incredibly too, the Northerners allowed the white rulers to get away with this legislation. Now, the colonial government after this success in the North was coming down to the Southern Nigeria to try its luck again but little did it know that it was in for ill-luck.

At Apapa in Lagos, the capital of Nigeria, there was a wide stretch of land belonging to the clan of which Chief Amodu Tijani Oluwa was the head. The Government decided to acquire about a square mile and a half, surrounded by a neutral zone a quarter of a mile wide, of this land for the purpose of providing allotments to European merchants. But what the government did not intend to do was pay the Chief or his family for this land as "owner" of it, but proposed to pay only for what was described as a "Seigneurial Right." (*See Seigneurial Right in SPECIAL MENTION on Page 155*) This amount came to £500 (Five hundred pound sterling) as compared to the worth of the land which was £22,000 (Twenty-two thousand pound sterling). This enlightened Chief found it insulting. Not only was he to be disposed of his natural possession, he was to be compensated with near to nothing. He resented this attempt to violate the principle of ownership in order to establish the Northern Nigeria system of placing native lands "at the disposal and under the control of the Governor." He sued the Secretary, Southern Provinces as provided for in the Sections 10 and 11 of the Public Land Ordinance No. 5 of 1903 under which his land was said to be required "for public purposes."

In the Supreme Court of Nigeria, the bases were loaded. He was taking his case to be judged by the very people whom he was fighting against. Obviously, he lost. But he didn't relent. He lodged an appeal in the Privy Council, the highest court on British land and herein came Herbert Heelas Macaulay, C.E., the Nigerian foremost Civil Engineer and politician familiar with land ownership and a thorn-in-the-flesh of the colonial government.

This case had already divided Nigeria. The Nigerian lapdogs of the colonialists, hankering after the British honorary titles of "Sirs," "Lords," "M.B.E," "C.M.G," etc., had swayed to the British side and supported the colonial government to the hilt but not so with people like Macaulay, defender of the native rights. He was asked to render his services to the Chief and he readily consented. A division between the Chief and the CE., was attempted when the pro-Government supporters tried to point out that the C.E. was a Christian and should not be supporting the Chief who was a muslim but this attempt at the division failed because Macaulay felt that he was supporting a Nigerian and a person who was being unjustly treated.

The Oluwa Landcase-1920
Leaving the Supreme Court in Lagos during the famous Oluwa Landcase are
from left to right: Herbert Macaulay (holding hat), Egerton Shyngle, Chief
Tijani Oluwa, and Yaya Oluwa (next to the Chief, his father)

On the 15th of May, 1920, the Chief left for England to pursue his case accompanied by Mr. Herbert Macaulay as his interpreter and Secretary. Now, herein entered the Eleko Affair. Oba Eshugbayi Eleko, the then Lagos reigning monarch who had ran afoul of the colonial government in a series of affairs, supported the Chief and gave his silver staff of Office which was presented to his great grandfather King Akintoye of Lagos by Queen Victoria on 1st of January, 1852, to Macaulay to show the British Government in Britain his gesture of support for the Chief. This action later caused a big problem because a lot of furor was made out of the staff.

In London, Solicitor Mr. E. F. Hunt appointed for Chief Oluwa, instructed Hon. Sir William Findlay, K.C., and Mr. J.A. Johnson the lawyers representing the Chief at the Council Chamber, Whitehall, London, S.W. in the presence of the following who presided over the case:

The Rt. Hon. Viscount Haldane, Rt. Hon. Lord Atkinson and The Rt. Hon. Lord Phillimore.

At the Privy Council, the case was heard for 5 days --the 6th, 7th, 8th, 9th, 20th, and 21st of June, 1921. On the 11th day of July 21, judgment was rendered by the Rt. Hon. Viscount Haldane in favor of the Chief. It was read thus: "The Appellant, Chief Oluwa, for the purposes of the Public Land Ordinance No.5 of 1903, is transferring to the Governor the land in question in 'full ownership'."

The Final Order was made on the 14th day of July, 1921, at the Court at Buckingham Palace at which were present, the King Most Excellent Majesty's Lord President, Lord Chamberlain. Also present were Lord Colebrooke, Lord Somerleyton and Sir Louis Davies.

In Lagos Pandemonium broke loose. Ten thousand Lagosians turned out on Thursday morning of the 25th of July, 1921, to welcome home Chief Oluwa and Herbert Macaulay in an incredibly rambunctious welcome home party at the landing stage by the Community of Lagos indigenes.

While in England, Chief Oluwa had the honor of attending the Army Officers Fete at the Royal Botanical Gardens in London where on the 24th of July, 1920, His Most Gracious Majesty King George the V shook hands with Chief Oluwa and chatted with the enlightened and intelligent Chief and at this auspicious occasion, Mr. Herbert Macaulay was the Chief's interpreter, holding the silver-mounted staff which was presented in 1852 to the King of Lagos by Her late Majesty Queen Victoria.

Now, even if Chief Oluwa had to part with part of his land whether willingly or unwillingly, he would be adequately compensated.

CHIEF AMODU TIJANI. THE OLUWA OF LAGOS.
AKOSA MAKO OGUN OBA.
WITH

HIS MAJESTY KING GEORGE V.
AT THE BOTANICAL GARDEN. LONDON ENGLAND

While in England, Chief Oluwa had the honor of attending the Army officers Fete at the Royal Botanical Gardens in London where on the 24th of July 1920, His Most Gracious Majesty King George the V shook hands with Chief Oluwa and chatted with the enlightened and intelligent Chief and at this auspicious occasion, Mr. Herbert Macaulay was the Chief's interpreter, holding the silver-mounted staff which was presented in 1852 to the King of Lagos by Her late Majesty Queen Victoria.

By the direction of the Privy Council judgment, the white Colonial Government of Nigeria paid Chief Oluwa in compensation £22,500 sterling.

The following was how the money was distributed:

1. £5,500 for the members of the Chief Oluwa family.
2. £4,900 deposited in the Bank for General Purpose.
3. £5,500 given personally to Chief Amodu Tijani Oluwa.
4. £4,517 refunded to Chief Oluwa for legal and other expenses while in England.
5. £2,083 to Herbert Macaulay as Private Secretary and Adviser to Chief Oluwa.
6. £600 as a personal gift to Herbert Macaulay by Chief Oluwa in kind appreciation of the Civil Engineer's invaluable services in the great Landcase.

Now, cold water has been poured over the blazing arrogance of power of the white government and as expected, there were resulting fall-outs including the following:

1. On Saturday the 8th of August, 1925, the Colonial Government deported to Oyo, Oba Eshugbayi Eleko.
2. On Monday 26th August, 1928, Mr. Herbert Macaulay was sent to prison for 6 months with hard labor for the Gunpowder Plot Rumor published in his daily newspaper the Lagos Daily News.
3. In 1944, The National Council of Nigeria and the Cameroons elected as its first President, Mr. Herbert Macaulay. From this position he planned a provincial tour of the party whose aim was to get a mandate of the people against the Richards Constitution and four ordinances which were popularly known as "Obnoxious" namely: Public Lands, Crown Lands, Minerals, and Appointment and Deposition of Chiefs Ordinances.
4. On October 1st 1960, the British Colonial rule in Nigeria came to an end. Nigeria became independent.

6

1920s-1930s
HOW JUJU MUSIC ACTUALLY OBTAINED ITS NAME

TOGO LAWSON •
IREWOLEDE DENGE •
SAMBA DRUM •
TUNDE KING •

After characters like Awerende, the new music that started with the tambourine and samba drum years later, in the beginning, was nameless. Notable among its players were Togo Lawson and Irewolede Denge. Togo Lawson was a dramatic character. A descendant of a family from the neighboring Togoland who had settled in Lagos long after the slavery days were over, he always went about the streets playing the tambourine (*More about Togo Lawson in SPECIAL MENTION on page 147*). He was not totally together because his behavior was somewhat erratic. Crew cut and frontal upper gap toothed, he was nearly always don in a khaki shirt with unbuttoned coverflaps and epaulets. To excite him, one only had to draw a line in his path and dare him to cross it. He wouldn't!. On the tambourine, he was superb. His famous compositions were *Awa o sise,* a song about the workers who refused to go back on duty when the colonial government refused to raise their pay, also *Sergeant Major Stoukas* and *Elemu* (The Palm-wine tapper). He switched to guitar when he formed a group. The other popular one was Irewolede Denge, an Ijebu Yoruba guitarist. His primary instrument was the framed rectangular shaped samba drum. He was tall, upright, neat and well spoken. His samba drumming and voice were unmistakable. At night, mostly by himself, people always loved to rush out of their houses to listen to his songs of love, philosophy, allegory etc., as he went along the streets. He too switched to guitar when he formed a group and started making recordings. His early recordings started on Odeon label in the 1920s. *Orin Asape Eko, Fija f'Olorun ja, Otutu ki meja,* were among those of his much loved early recordings that Lagosians loved to sing.

Irewolede Denge came to Lagos from Ijebu-Ode to find work as a laborer. Initially, he resided at Oshodi Street in the Epetedo neighborhood of Lagos. In the daytime, he worked as a laborer and in the evening, to supplement his income, he usually made rounds singing accompanied by his framed rectangular samba drum. He always started his journey from Oshodi Street and sometimes walked down to Tokunboh Street, turned into Andrew Street, entered Ricca Street and eventually to Odunfa Street. At the beginning of Odunfa Street where Tokunboh and Massey Streets took off, Denge on some nights turned left into Tokunboh Street and headed back towards the Epetedo area. On other nights when he turned right, he always walked towards Massey Street. When the mood grabbed him on the nights he turned towards Massey Street, he usually quickly made another sharp turn to the left into Carrena Street and headed towards Bangbose, Kakawa and Campbell Streets and Igbosere Road. On these streets were located houses of some Lagos's "big guns" as far as riches were concerned and Denge was in the mood that might to draw some money out of their pockets. Candido da Rocha, the Lagos's mythical millionaire, Doctors Adefolu and Majekodunmi, Saka Tinunbu, Joseph Saveyan Branco, Ladipo Anjou, Magistrate Abayomi to name a few, all lived on these streets and Denge always sang for them all. By the time he returned home, his shorts' pockets were always full of money.

Later he switched to guitar and started making recordings. He also formed a group as he was getting older. His early recordings were on Odeon label and his late recordings were on Ogunde label.

When Denge was getting older, he developed throat problem. He moved from Oshodi Street to Ije a quieter and more down-to-earth area surrounded by vegetation and river, behind Obalende

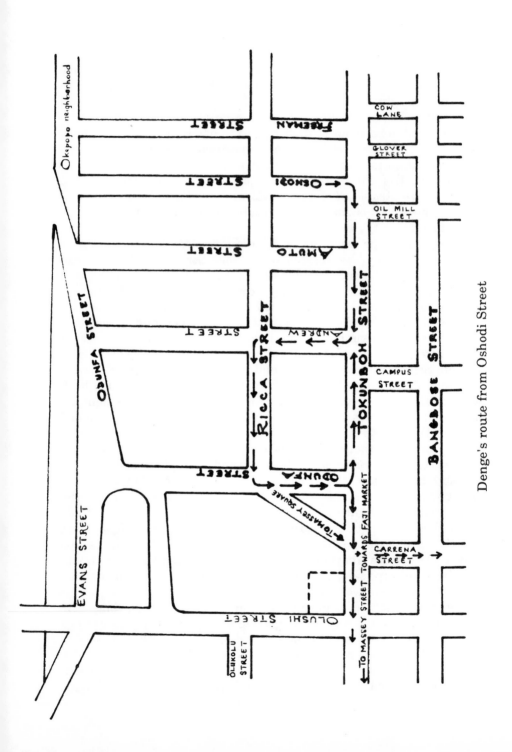

Denge's route from Oshodi Street

Tokunboh Street, Lagos.

Odunfa Street, Lagos.

neighborhood known at that time as the Lagos "boondocks" where nobody wanted.   This did not put abatement   to his ailment. Eventually, he was moved to the General Hospital at Marina for treatment. There, he died.

As the music started to gain in popularity minstrelsy graduated to duos and combos. By the 1930s, social demand like naming ceremony, wedding, graduation ceremony parties, funerals etc., in which celebrants needed musicians to juice up the occasions, started to make the music more popular and caused increase in the size of people and instruments used in playing it.

Added to the original tambourine and samba drum were sekere (gourd rattle) and various string instruments like guitar, banjo, ukulele or mandoline. In the mid 1930s, a turn-about came to the music.

Tunde King, the old king of juju music

A gentleman by the name of 'Tunde King, a Yoruba, who was born in Lagos in 1910 and who had been associated with this music, formed his own ensemble. This was in 1932 (*More on Tunde King in MILESTONES on page 122*). His original team included a samba drummer. To get a better taste of this new music, he decided to add the tambourine. At the Salvation Army store, he procured one and gave it to his samba drummer. The samba drummer developed a style with the instrument. During or at the tail-end of a good number, he usually threw or tossed the tambourine up in the air and caught it much to the ovation and approval of the onlookers or dancers. Now, the word "ju" in the Yoruba language means toss or throw. Accented with the upward and downward strokes "ju ju" for its tossing up and coming down, the tonal motion gave juju its name. The particular word was the action of the samba drummer and it was the onlookers who gave it to the music as its name. The tambourine from then on also became known as juju. Not only that, when Tunde made some recordings in 1936 on Parlophone label, he was the first artist to designate juju as the music's name on the label. Contrary to popular belief, Tunde King did not invent juju music and he didn't invent the name either. The octogenarian who was honest enough to give this account of the christening of the music was also instrumental in establishing the definitive number of juju music players of four, which was standard for a longtime. This second theory of the naming of juju music is the most plausible of a debatable three. However, buffs of Nigerian music can easily tear into the action of Tunde's samba drummer as unoriginal. In the 4th century, long before juju came into being, Ayan, the drummer of a Yoruba king in Oyo, who invented various types of drums (to be played for special types of occasions) like Adamo, Gudugudu, Konongo, Omele, Bata, Bembe, Gbedu, Lukorigi etc., played the gangan music which is one of the oldest and early African musics. Players of this music usually consisted of one lead drummer (Iyalu) and between five to ten other gangan drummers of various sizes and shapes of gangan drums, serving as rhythm and backing players. As time passed, a sekere (gourd rattle) player was added and later, an aro (giant steel bracelets with sonorous high pitch sound) player was finally added. This became standard of gangan music group. At the end of a good number, a gourd-rattler, sensing the good mood of the dancers and onlookers joyfully usually threw the gourd-rattle up in the air and caught it to show his pleasure. On some occasions like this, he was usually pinned on his forehead coins for appreciation. The samba drummer probably took his cue from there. The gangan music could be heard on many Nigerian social occasions and on some ceremonies and plays such as Egungun, Eyo, Gelede, Alapafuja, Agere, Igunnu, Agemo etc. On the crowning of a king or chief, the bugle is added for novelty.

A third theory of the name of the music came from the sound that the tambourine emits when hit or slapped by the fingers or palm. The original juju's rhythmic sound from the tambourine was the four short and quick ju-gbu- ju-gbu and the two last ju-ju with tonal

THE NAMING OF JUJU MUSIC
Toss

"JU" in the Nigeria's Yoruba tribal language means toss or throw. The action of tossing the tambourine up and catching it, and the duplication of the word ju, give juju music its name.

Parlophone record

Parlophone label
*In 1936, on Parlophone label, the type above, was where the name
"JUJU" first appeared on the recordings of 'Tunde King.*

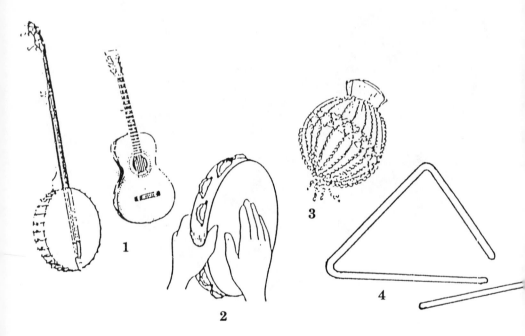

Tunde's instruments (Combo)

*Tunde's group consisted of (1) guitar-banjo, (2) tambourine,
(3) sekere, (4) triangle or cymbals – a format that all juju groups at
that time copied and which became a standard.*

accent on the two. A complete sequence is jú-gbú-jú-gbú-jùjú. The tonal emphasis on the last two was said by some to have given juju its name.

The 1930s saw many juju musicians like Ayinde Bakare, Ojo Babajide, S.S. Peters and Akanbi Ege to name a few, making recordings on HMV, Parlophone and Odeon labels. This particular decade was also the decade of both urban and imported competitors.

Tunde's combo which consisted of guitar-banjo (himself on guitar and vocals) tambourine (juju) sekere (gourd-rattle) cymbals or triangle (doubling as second vocal) became a standard format copied by all juju musicians of the 1930s.

OCCASIONS WHERE GANGAN MUSIC CAN BE HEARD

THE GANGAN MUSIC

The gangan music could be heard on many Nigerian social occasions, and on some ceremonies and plays such as Egungun, Eyo, Gelede, Alapafuja, Agere, Igunnu, Agemo, etc. On the crowning of a king or installation of a chief, the bugle is added for novelty.

Ganga music players
Young Gangan music players master the art form youth.
(Note the gourd rattler fifth from left)

Young Gangan music players rendering their services at a social
occasion.

OCCASIONS WHERE GANGAN MUSIC CAN BE HEARD

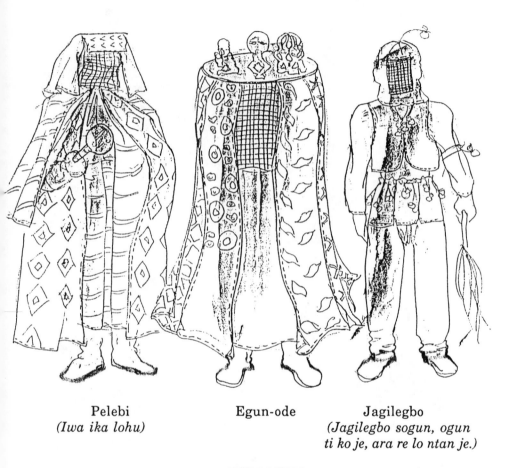

Pelebi	Egun-ode	Jagilegbo
(Iwa ika lohu)		*(Jagilegbo sogun, ogun ti ko je, ara re lo ntan je.)*

EGUNGUN
(Ara orun kenken)

Egungun play is a play usually staged for the spirit of the departeds. One of the early appearances of Egungun masquerade in Lagos was in 1775 during the reign of King Adele Ajosun. It was his children that introduced this play from the palace in opposition to the religion of Mohamedanism that had just arrived and which was the first imported religion in Lagos. Civil war broke out over this and the King had to go into exile after suffering defeat. He later regained his throne.

OCCASIONS WHERE GANGAN MUSIC CAN BE HEARD

EYO
(*The Adamu-Orisa play*)

EYO
(*The Adamu-Orisa play*)

The most loved of all masquerade plays is the Adamu-Orisa. It is a play in remembrance of any Lagos eminent personality that had died but who had contributed morally, socially or politically toward the development of the country. On only one occasion, it was staged for the visit of Queen Elizabeth II of England to Nigeria in 1956.

The player wears a felt hat and robe. His face is covered with gauzed cloth and he carries a staff known as Opanbata which he gently touches upon meeting with somebody he knows.

The Adamu-Orisa play was introduced into Lagos from Ibefun by Ojo Oniyun to celebrate the death of Erelu-Kuti the mother of Kuno Ologunkutere. (*Today, Ojo Oniyun has a street named after him at Ebute-Metta, just behind Apapa Road in Lagos.*) Erelu-Kuti was the sister of King Akinsemoyin (1704-1749). She volunteered to marry Alagba, the King's Ifa priest when all of the king's daughters refused to be betrothed to the priest.

The first group of Eyos in Lagos were very few. They were called Olori-Eyo (leaders of the Eyos). They were also known as the Alaketepupa (*The Redhats*) or Langalanga. They carried Laba, the Royal standard and their hats were red with Langalanga inscribed on the front side of their hats. Later, the play developed and other Lagos chiefs joined in the celebration.

A couple of days before the celebration starts, an announcement of the play is heralded by the Awo Osugbo Akala, who goes about in the streets in his ancient and traditional dresses.

On the day of the celebration, the Oniko representing the god, goes out first at 2:30 a.m. to pay his respect to the symbolic corpse lying in state.

The symbolic corpse is an imaginary image of the dead person that is laid in state for the occasion. After Oniko, another representative of another god, the Adimu follows, then all of the Eyos follow, paying their respect to the symbolic corpse, and go to Agodo, a special enclosure where they sing and dance. The entrance of Agodo is opened with Opanbata and an Eyo without a ticket is not allowed in.

All Eyos pay traditional obeisance to Adimu by lowering their Opanbata. The Eyos have their traditional superstitions too. For example, an Eyo never crosses a bridge. It is also widely believed in Lagos that after an Adamuorisa play, there will be peace and prosperity in the whole country.

OCCASIONS WHERE GANGAN MUSIC CAN BE HEARD

GELEDE

A play staged possibly to salute a newly appointed chief. The masquerader wears a woman's head mask. His chest is heavily padded to give appearance of large bosoms and the over emphasized buttocks are effected by rolled wall fotomat. The ankles are covered with noisy metal bangles that jingle as we walks along. The appearance of a Gelede is a mimicry of the feminine gender.

OCCASIONS WHERE GANGAN MUSIC CAN BE HEARD

ALAPAFUJA

A unique masquerade whose purpose of play is somewhat obscure. Its last public appearance was in the early 1960s. The masquerader, a partially deaf and speech impaired gentleman if either dead or retired by now probably has nobody to carry on the tradition.

He is enclosed in a wooden mask comprising of a head, neck and torso with arms that are perpetually stretched out horizontally.

OCCASIONS WHERE GANGAN MUSIC CAN BE HEARD

AGERE
Stilt dancer that performs during some muslim festivals and also
sometimes to welcome the arrival of a New Year.

OCCASIONS WHERE GANGAN MUSIC CAN BE HEARD

IGUNNU
Seen sometimes in the morning or by night, the play is more cultish than fetish. It was said to be originally brought to Lagos by the Nupes who used it for witch hunting.

OCCASIONS WHERE GANGAN MUSIC CAN BE HEARD

AGEMO

AGEMO

Agemo is an annual fetish masquerade play associated with the Ijebus. The presence of the masquerade in the streets signals the arrival of rainy season that ushers in the ripeness and harvesting of corn-on-the-cob, the freshness of which is to be celebrated. Of all the Ijebu towns, only seven viz: Odogebolu, Imushin, Okun, Imosan, Ago-Iwoye, Isiwo and Oru have Agemos. At Imosan, seventeen Agemo masquerades representing the seven towns congregate annually to lead in the celebration. Oba Awujale of Ijebu-Ode always donate a cow to slaughter for sacrifice. Human beings used to be slaughtered for sacrifice in the old days. The colonial government put a stop to that practice.

Agemo is of two types. One, enclosed in a rolled mat and unseen and the other, seen, naked to the waist with the lateral half of his body painted in colors. He shakes a gourd-rattle as he goes in the streets. Women are forbidden to look at Agemo.

Agemo is the name that the Yorubas also give to the praying-mantis. When it treads, the jerky movement with its somewhat dance-like appearance makes the Yoruba to say to an offspring who cannot follow in his or her parent's footsteps that: "The praying-mantis has given birth to its offspring, lack of ability to dance is up to the offspring." In other words, shame on you if your parents are good at something and you completely lack the ability to do that thing. Or to put it in another way: "I've done my share, the rest is up to you."

7

POPULAR TYPES OF MUSIC

EXISTENCE OF SOME OTHER TYPES OF POPULAR MUSIC BEFORE JUJU

SAKARA •

"STEAMING" •

ASIKO •

AJAYI "KOBOKO" •

PALM WINE •

AMBROSE CAMPBELL •

Areas which settlers congregated and ethnic compositions in Lagos, had a great deal of effect on juju and other types of music.

The first Lagos settlers, the Yorubas from Ile-Ife who became the indigenes, congregated or settled at Isale Eko by the Lagos Lagoon where the king's palace, the Iga Iduganran was built. The Isale Eko area encompassed Idumagbo, Ebute Ero and Itolo.

As the name implies in the Yoruba language, Isale Eko is, the bottom of Lagos (*Isale-bottom Eko-Lagos*) or downtown of Lagos. In fact, that area is actually the uptown because just by its edge is the bridge that leads to the mainland and the outskirts of Lagos when one is saying "good-bye" to the city.

After abolition of slavery, the liberated slaves that found their ways back home from Freetown in Sierra Leone, and also the countries of Liberia and Gambia, came and settled in the areas of Marina, Tinubu and Olowogbowo, the midtown of Lagos. They were variously known as Saro and the repatriates. They came back still bearing the english names of their slave masters. These were the second settlers.

Lagos was made the capital of the colonial Nigeria in 1914. Before then, people from the various tribal kingdoms of what was later to be gathered together to make a whole country of Nigeria began moving to this bursting city and notable were the Nupes from the North who settled at Lafiaji, the downtown of Lagos. They were attracted to this area because it was a marshland of swamp suitable for rice growing, their specialty. These were the third settlers.

Aroloya, Anikantamo, Faji and Massey Square areas, the eastward midtown of Lagos, provided havens for the fourth settlers.

Between 1854 and 1859, the Portuguese liberated slaves settled in the areas of Bangbose, Campus, Igbosere and upwards to Cow Lane, the downtown of Lagos. Surnames of these settlers were usually the Spanish and Portuguese names of DaSilva, Domingo, Vera-Cruz, Gomez, Pereira, Hernandez, Fernandez etc., etc. They were Catholic Christians. These were the fifth settlers.

By 1862 to 1868, the sixth and last settlers arrived at Epetedo not far from Cow Lane and Oshodi area. Epetedo was aptly named for notable civil war returnees that were exiled in Epe. Further down behind Epetedo were Obalende, Ikoyi and Victoria Island. These areas were later inhabited by emigrants from the Gold Coast (Ghana), Dahomey, and the Ijaws of Nigeria. When the township cemetery at Igbosere Road (Ite oku Igboro) was finally filled, Ikoyi was the type of place that the colonial government probably had in mind with reference to the part of Article VIII of the treaty signed with the king of Lagos that went:

> ......*The Obas and the Chiefs of Lagos further agree to set apart a piece of land, within a convenient distance of the principal towns, to be used as burial ground for Christian persons. And the funerals and sepulchers of the dead shall not be disturbed in any way or upon any account.*

Now, how did these areas that the settlers inhabited and the ethnic composition in Lagos affected juju and other types of music. Firstly, it should be borne in mind that people from other towns of Nigeria apart from these settlers also came and settled in some other parts of Lagos. They came to find jobs as laborers, shipping clerks, etc., etc. Secondly, beginning from 1910, minstrels using

tambourine and the framed rectangular samba drum had started to
invent a type of music which had no particular name to it. Among
some of these minstrels were Togo Lawson, born in Lagos and
Irewolede Denge who came to find job in Lagos as a laborer from the
town of Ijebu-Ode and who lived at Oshodi Street, the downtown area
of Lagos. Popular music around this time included Sakara,
"Steaming" the forerunner of Highlife, Asiko and Palmwine.

Sakara music consisted of the calabash bowl (Igba Sakara), Goje,
Ofa and the one face drum peg-fastened with a series of opa sticks.
The round body is made of earthenware, the native ceramic. All of
the musical instruments used in playing the sakara music were
conspicuous because they were all native to Nigeria.

The centerpiece of attraction however was the igba sakara, the
calabash bowl played faced down. The player usually had rings on
the second fingers of both hands so as to give the characteristic
rasping sound when the bowl was tapped or hit. The Goje usually
started off the music with a few bass on the instrument, then the
calabash, the drum, the ofa (bow) and all the vocal elements of the
band joined in. When this music became popular in Lagos in 1920,
it was first played by a gentleman named Bello Tapa from Northern
Nigeria who lived around the areas of Lafiaji and Epetedo. He was
a muslim and not educated. In time, the music became
synonymous with the area, the settlers of the area and the muslims--
the religious group of the founder. This was how area of the settlers
and ethnic composition, affected music in Lagos. When the
playing of the music spread and began to be dominated by the
Western Nigerian Yorubas, it did not lose its grip of where it drew
its origin. Great exponents of the music included Abibu Oluwa,
Salami "Lefty" Balogun and some others. Salami was a drummer
in the Abibu Oluwa's group. He was a southpaw hence the
nickname "Lefty". It was when Abibu died that he formed his own
group.

Another famous music of the time was "steaming", popularized
by Calabar Brass Band and also known as the Lagos Mozart
Orchestra. The band consisted of trumpets, tubas, trombones and
marching drums of snares, sides and base. Because of its western
influence, the band was always patronized by Lagosians western
educated elites who always needed it for weddings, public parties
and other social occasions. Their leader, a gentleman by the name
of Asuquo Bassey together with some other members of the band,
hailed from the Eastern Nigerian town of Calabar hence the band's
name but Lagos being what it was, a tinge of Yoruba had to manifest

in anything to be able to sell. This was why it was no wonder at all when the band's hit record was the Yoruba one that went thus:

Ore mi kini se, kini se
(My friend why, why)
To fi nsa lo fiafia
(Are you running away in a hurry)
Sa lo e, sa lo e, sa lo e
(Running away, running away, running away)
To fi nsa lo fiafia
(Are you running away in a hurry)

This music was the forerunner of the highlife music of the late 1940s, the 1950s and half of the 1960s.

The Asiko was the music that was competing in popularity with Sakara music. It had everything in opposition to Sakara in that it was played by Christians and by youngsters. It was faster in beat than Sakara. It's instrumentations were about five rectangular samba drums of various sizes, a carpenter's saw and a bottle and nail to supply timing. Asiko was the forerunner of Konkoma music that came to Lagos via Lome and the Gold Coast (Ghana) in the 1940s. Services of Asiko music were usually rendered on Christmas Day, Easter festivities, social and public parties etc. Players of Asiko music were originally from the Lafiaji area and because they were Christians and of the repatriates extractions, this music was common with the Christians and the Saros.

Fierce competition from young men in various areas or neighborhoods of Lagos that formed their own Asiko groups always made them to assume fanciful and dramatic second names or aliases possibly for intimidation purposes. For instance a group's leader by the name of Amusa was more known by his alias of "Captain." Samu Egbo was also known as Samu "Esu" (Samu "the Devil") (Samu, short for Samuel) and Ajayi Williams was known as Ajayi "Koboko" (Ajayi "the whip").   They probably might as well resorted to these aliases because if competition did not produce threats from opposing Asiko music groups from other areas, there were threats from other sources not related to music. Invariably, each area had its own bullies and leaders of groups such as fancy, caretta, sailors, cowboys, fanti and raffia masquerades (egun oniko) that turned out on festive occasions and paraded the streets and who could foment trouble at the least irritation just to show "bigness".

These bullies or leaders had intimidating aliases too and memorable were "Tiger" Pedro, S. "Tanko" Kuti of Campus Square, "Longus" of Isale Eko, Faustineau and "Sigidi" Pabo of Ricca Street area to name a few. Some of these bullies have been known to waylay masquerades, break myths, expose cult secrets, etc., when they felt that they had been disrespected or when they wanted attention.

Recordings of Asiko music was made by Asiko music players such as A.B.O. Mabinuori, Amusa "Captain" with his group boys Jero, Bangbose, Daniel and Dawodu Mabinuori. Other famous Asiko players included Samu Egbo, Ajayi Williams, Alabi Labilu and Tesilimi. Asiko songs memorialized important events in Lagos, two most famous were the arrival of the first aeroplane in Lagos in 1928 and the piteous event of Doctor Adeniyi-Jones, a Saro house owner and medical practitioner who went to collect rent from a poor crew-man tenant but had the ill-luck of meeting the tenant in a bad mood. An argument ensued over which this tenant drew a machete and caused blood to flow.

The song went thus:
Dokita to wale sinwo
(The doctor who came to collect rent)
Krumo binu f'ada yo
(Crew-man got angry and drew machete)
E wa w'eje ni Lafiaji
(Come and see blood at Lafiaji (area))
The song memorializing the event of the first aircraft that arrived in Lagos in 1928 went thus:
London n'ilu oba
(London is the city of the King (British King))
Bonfo ma ba e lo
(If you're flying, I will go with you)

Another popular music of this time was the palmwine; so called because the music could be largely heard in clubs where palm-wine was usually served without limitation. The music could be heard in bars along marina area enjoyed by sailors and crew-men, the chief clientels. The most popular group that played this music was the Nigerian Jolly Boys Orchestra. The string instrumentalists of this group were superbly adroit players who usually left no doubt about their adroitness when they performed. This in turn earned them respect and recording contract from good and established recording company. The band consisted of Thomas Omotajo, Akanbi Bale, Ambrose Campbell, Abiodun Oke also known as Brewster Hughes, Sunday "Harbor Giant," and Coffie Mando all working-class immigrants of Saro, Kru, Ashanti and Yoruba extractions. Their instruments were three guitars, one mandoline, one samba drum, one triangle and a pennywhistle.

Their leader Sunday "Harbor Giant" was a Kru sailor and he played the pennywhistle.

The band recorded many hit songs including <u>F.B. Godo</u> (a popular Lagos elite), <u>In The Public Interest Of The Boys -HMV.J17</u> and <u>Atari Ajanaku</u>. Atari Ajanaku was their biggest hit. From the ongoing, it would be seen that areas of settlers and ethnic composition dictated the type of music that these people played and the type of people that patronized them.

By the time that the World War II broke out, all of the elements of this group vanished. After the World War II, only two of them resurfaced, this time in London, England. The two were Ambrose Campbell and Brewster Hughes. A Nigerian hotelier had acquired a night spot on Wardour Street at the Soho Square's West End section of London and called it Club Afrique. He engaged the services of Ambrose Campbell, a skilled guitarist and good singer who then formed a band and called it the West African Rhythm Brothers. Elements of the band included Nigerians and West Indians such as Ade Bashorun (Bongos & congas) who once played with Ayinde Bakare, Oladipo Anjou, Oni Pedro, Abiodun Oke (who later branched and formed Nigerian Union Rhythm Group) Hipolyte, Ginger Ishola Folorunsho, all Nigerians and Willy Roachford (Alto sax and clarinet) and Adams (Trumpet) the last two from the West Indies. The band secured a good recording contract with Emile Shalit owner of Melodisc Records. When their records started to find their ways to Nigeria, every single one was a hit. The music of this band did not sound like the palmwine's Jolly Orchestra. The West African Rhythm Brothers Band was a big band with horns and a rhythm section. Its music was the popular highlife. Around that time in London, African bands that played similar style included Nat Atkins and his Crazy Bees of Ghana and Rans Boi and his Group also of Ghana. Ambrose remained in London for years and it was not until twenty to twenty-five years later when Nigeria got its Independence from Britain did Ambrose step again on the native soil of his motherland of Nigeria. Today, he is in his eighties, retired.

Ambrose Campbell

Ambrose Campbell and The West African Rhythm Brothers Band

HISTORY OF JUJU MUSIC

8

1930s -1940s

GVs, FOREIGN MUSIC •
WORLD WAR II •
PICKUPS & P.A.SYSTEMS •
AYINDE BAKARE •

By the 1930s, juju music had overtaken sakara, asiko,parade and palmwine types of music in popularity. While sakara was still hanging on, asiko, palmwine and parade were ebbing away fastly. The reason was not hard to figure out. Players of some of these other types of music wanted to move with the tide. For instance, Sunday "Harbor Giant", leader of the Nigerian Jolly Boys Orchestra had decided to stop playing the palmwine music and to form a juju group. Alabi Labilu who lived around the Lafiaji area and who was a great exponent of Asiko music had decided to form a juju group too. This was in 1934. Among his boys was a gentleman who played the group's samba drum. This samba drummer later became a nationally famous juju band leader and guitarist who made history in juju music—his name, Ayinde Bakare (more on him later). There were also the following: Olu Ogunrombi and

Akanbi Wright from Olowogbowo area, Ladipo Esugbayi from Isale Eko, Tunji Banjo from Ebute Metta and from outside of Lagos, Ojo Babajide from Ibadan and Theophilus Iwalokun from Okitipupa to name a few.

Ayinde Bakare

By the late 1930s and spilling into the 1940s, urban competitors like parade music, and foreign music like *son* or *sonsonette* known as G.V. from Cuba with the Sexteto Habanero, playing compositions of Metamoros, dominated the Lagos music market. There were also Calypso from the West Indies and Fanti music from the Gold Coast. As the Lagosians were enjoying life more abundantly the World War II broke out (*see Ogun Ajakaiye Keji in*

A WHOLE SCENE GOING on Page 79) and it had a big effect on juju music which had graduated from its ensemble stature to big band size with the introduction of more instruments into it like cowbell, talking drum (gangan or adamo), conga drum, bongos and claves. Konkoma, a type of music from the Gold Coast was a strong competitor.

The war affected Lagos to the point that food was rationed, there was control on home produce and profiteering became an offense punishable by stiff jail terms. People who were able to leave the country left and went overseas and many young men joined the army. Eventually, Germany was defeated and the war was over in 1945. When the war was over, some other turnabouts immediately came to juju music. Advancement in western technology was one. Nigerian musicians exposed to western formats during their stay overseas and who came back home after the war, started to use Public Address System (PA System), speakers, electronic amplification in general. Juju borrowed from these and it was the start of electric guitars, amplifiers and speakers in juju music. Without ever knowing he was making history, in 1949, Ayinde Bakare was the first juju artist to use the western technology of electronic amplification. The small size of his ukulele-banjo made it impossible to accommodate a pick-up so he switched to guitar and attached the pick-up to it. With the electric guitar, the 1940s format was tambourine, sekere, cowbell, gangan, conga, bongos and claves. Among popular artists around this time were Akanbi Ege, Julius Olofin, 'Tunde Nightingale, Ojoge Daniel, Njemanze and Ojindo.

A WHOLE SCENE GOING
OGUN AJAKAIYE KEJI

CHAPTER 8
SUB-CHAPTER 8:1

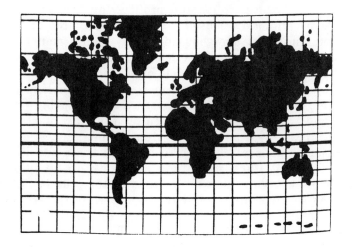

HITLER •
MUSSOLINI •
SELASSIE •
NIGERIAN REGIMENT •
AKANBI WRIGHT •

Ogun Ajakaiye Keji means World War II. This war was so named because it affected in one way or another all the nations on the face of the earth and nearly the whole world participated in it either directly or indirectly. By the 1930s, with very few exception of fearless, highly educated African dissenters against colonial rule in the British colonies, the whole of the West African countries under the British rule had developed a morbid loyalty to Great Britain.

'Tunde King, the juju king had made a record in 1936 in honor of King George, called "Oba Oyinbo" in which he affectionately called the British monarch "our father". The Lagos colonial government had declared every May 24, "EMPIRE DAY" in which athletes from various colonial government accredited elementary schools compete in various track and field events to win a trophy in form of a big shield for their schools.

Adolf Hitler (The Furher)

When World War II broke out, the colonial governor of the Gold Coast (now Ghana) touring its Northern Territories in 1943 visited the Builsas, a remote tribe with warrior traditions. At a colorful ceremony, he was welcomed by Azantilow, Chief of Sandema who had raised a full battalion for service with the Royal West African Frontier Force.

In a tribute to Britain, the Chief said "The English have been here for a long time now. We remember how things were before you came. We know what you have done, and we thank you.

Benito Mussolini (The Duce)

Now, for the sake of you we are safe, and because you live, we live. The English who are in Europe are fighting to save us from trouble. If we are asked for help, we give it willingly, for we do not want a stranger to come and rule us." Such was the morbid loyalty to Britain in all of the West African colonies. When Nazi leader, Adolf Hitler started the war, included in his many reasons for so doing were: the return which he wanted, of the German territories that were taken from Germany after his country lost the World War

I; the lift of the economic sanctions that were imposed on Germany which sent the country into a state of depression causing joblessness and strife; domination and profiteering of trade which he claimed were caused by the jews.

Erwin Rommel (The Desert Fox)

Africa was not his priority but change of things brought him to the continent when he had to send one of his favorite war generals Erwin Rommel to North Africa. His ally, fascist, Benito Mussolini who was "much talk, less fight" leader of Italy had bungled things up for him. Britain, knowing the military capabilities of Italy warned Mussolini not to go into war but Africa, he thought, was too much of an easy price for him to ignore. Until Dunkirk, West Africa had been largely a spectator but for the first time in the

Second World War, it went into battle against Italy. In Abyssinia, the Africans won glowing tributes for their efficiency and courage.

The Nigerian Regiment took part in the spectacular advance to Harar, covering over 1,000 miles in 30 days. The Gold Coast Regiment won an important victory in the South by their fierce assault on Wadara.

Emperor Haile Selassie (The Lion of Juda)

At Aduwa, the Ethiopians (then Abyssinians) handed out one of the worst defeats to an ill-equipped Italian infantry to the embarrassment of Italy.

With the fall of France, the West African Colonies found themselves flanked by potentially hostile territory. Defence communications had to be increased, and much larger West African Frontier Force (WAFF) had to be built up, housed and fed.

In November 1942, West Africa entered a new phase in its war effort. The WAFF was built up into the largest expeditionary force ever sent out by the British Colonies to fight the growing Japanese menace in India.

In July 1943, the first West African unit landed in India. By mid-1944 a volunteer army almost 100,000 strong, consisting of the 81st and 82nd (West African) Divisions and full supporting troops of all arms, was in action against Japan.

In 1945, the 81st and 82nd Divisions scored great victories in the Arakan hills on the Indo-Burma frontier, the victories which, with those of the 14th Army, culminated in the liberation of Burma and the recapture of Rangoon. The 81st became the first Division in South-East Asia to be supplied entirely by air.

A Nigerian Brigade was detached to form part of Major-General Wingate's famous CHINDITS, fighting for months on end behind the Japanese lines. "Black Commandos" from the 81st Divisions Reconnaissance Regiment made over 100 waterborne raids behind the enemy on the Arakan coastal front.

In defence and attack, fighting continually under appalling conditions, West African troops showed themselves to be well adapted to jungle mobile warfare. "The solid value of the African, is his absolute undefeated cheerfulness" said a Staff Officer, afterwards.

✳❂✳❂✳❂✳❂✳❂✳❂✳❂✳❂✳❂✳❂✳❂✳

Arinu rode Olukore, gbope was o Baba
(He, who sees the inside and outside Lord of the harvest, accept our offerings O Father)
Arinu rode Olukore, gbope wa o Baba
(He, who sees the inside and outside Lord of the harvest, accept our offerings O Father)
Jek'ogun ko pari o
(Let the war finish)
Kote ko dopin o
(Acrimony to come to an end)
Kale jaiye wa o baba
(So that we can enjoy our lives O Father)
Gbope wa o baba
(Accept our thanks, O Father)

The above was a song, sang in a Harvest and Thanksgiving mass at a church in Lagos, during the World War II. The effect of the war could be noticed in the wordings of the song. All over the continent of Africa, for both young and old, singularly or collectively, tense was the atmosphere. The participation of the black race in the war was immense but sad to say, ignored in the annals of its history.

About 22 episodes covering the beginning to the end of the war in a television program called WORLD AT WAR, written by Neal Ascherson, directed by Hug Raggett with narration supplied by Sir Laurence Olivier was made, but not a single episode was devoted to tell of the exploits and heroism of the black race during the war. It was when somebody dug out the films of their incredible war efforts in archives, where they had been jettisoned and forgotten and exposed the cruelty of the neglect, that a special program on black soldiers in the war was televised. The derision that they went through as if they were the enemies, was unheard of in human history.

In the United States of America, when African Americans started registering in the U.S. army to participate in the war, efforts were made to prevent them from combat duty. According to the television program, the African Americans were said to be black people and they had no right to shoot at the Germans, the enemies, who were white people!

When France was besieged and needed help of any kind at all costs, it asked for the "rejects" of America. It was not until the blacks proved their worth in France were they allowed to fight side by side with their white comrades in their nation's army from America. Their heaviest war decorations for appreciation did not come from their country of birth. They came from France which was eternally grateful to them. Worse was, they were even segregated in restaurants when the war was over.

A similar incident happened out of Africa too, and juju music made sure to never let the nation concerned forget it. It was in Nigeria. The British Royal Air Force (RAF) had been a bastion of the British elites, copper-tight and well beyond the comprehension of egalitarian mass. After some Nigerians were trained and found ready and competent to fly sorties, the British decided not to use their services. On what grounds was this decision based? According to the British, the Africans were potential carriers of malaria and God forbade if their blue bloods were contaminated! Thanks to the nationalistic movement in Nigeria around this time. They found this allegation very insulting and their protest did not let up until five Nigerian trainees were admitted into the R.A.F. Admirable was the heroism of Ace P.J.C. Thomas who showed everybody that what the white people could do, took little effort to accomplish on the part of the blacks if and when given the chance. Akanbi Wright (Akanbi Ege later) a juju band leader of the time who was very nationalistic, made a record called _The Five Nigerian R.A.F._ in remembrance of these five men. He also made some other records deriding Hitler which were popular and which the British had no qualms about using to drum up support for their war efforts throughout the nation of Nigeria.

The war in Burma which was fought mostly in the Burmese jungle was the most trying assignment for the Nigerians but sad to say Her Majesty, the Queen of England, Queen Elizabeth's favorite uncle, Lord Mountbatten who was the Field Marshal in charge of the Burma operations did not say anything about the heroism of these Nigerians.   However, during her visit to Nigeria in 1956, the Queen did lay a wreath at the Idumota Cenotaph, the monument that commemorates the heroism of Nigerian soldiers that died in World War I. In that thick Burmese jungle where the air was too thick to breath, where tree tops made perpetual canopies that caused day long darkness, where every step was into marshlands filled with leeches, poisonous snakes and other dangerous reptiles that drag on their chests, where scorpions and spiders all abide, they fought, died, and some survived and returned home. Nothing was said about them. Thanks to juju music which memorialized some of these events.

When the war was over, most of the Germans who perpetrated atrocities in Europe during the war were hunted down, prosecuted and hanged for war crimes. Those that escaped and living today are still being hunted down in order to be brought to face justice. Now, what about the atrocities that the Italians perpetrated on the Ethiopians? A number cannot be put on these Africans that the Italians ruthlessly disemboweled, publicly hanged, mercilessly slaughtered, shamelessly butchered, needlessly left in streets to rot with a large number, carelessly dumped in mass open graves. Most of the officers in the Italian army that committed these crimes are still living and whenever anybody goes into the war archives to dig out their names, expose them and have them prosecuted for war crimes, there are always efforts to block this attempt both from the United Kingdom and the United States of America. And here we go again. What is good for the whites is not good for the blacks.

The Queen of England, Her Majesty, Queen Elizabeth the II's visit to Nigeria in 1956.

HISTORY OF JUJU MUSIC

9

1940s–1950s
POST-WAR JUJU
MUSIC INSTRUMENTS

THE PALM-WINE TAPPERS •
ADEOLU •
AGIDIGBO •
KOKORO •

I LA is a Yoruba town in the western part of Nigeria. A steady influx of folks of this town to Lagos around the 1940s made popular a musical instrument associated with them. Known as elemu, (*palmwine seller*), palmwine tapping was their specialty. Sundown always brought them together, drinking the unsold leftovers and engaging in communal singing accompanied by this instrument. The musical instrument is known as Agidigbo.

Agidigbo is basically a rectangular box with a round hole like that of a guitar, located on one of its six faces. Over the hole lie five or six steel bands cut to various lengths for the purpose of graduation in pitch and held down at first ends with the second ends free. The free ends of the steel bands are those that are plucked with the thumb and the rest of the

Palm-wine tappers

fingers. Agidigbo cannot be tuned. The length of the steels determine their notes and the notes are definitive. A short steel when plucked emits a high note and a long steel emits a low note. It is hard to play a melody on this instrument. Its best advantage lies in rhythm and improvisation.

In the 1950s, a young man by the name of Adeolu Akinsanya from Abeokuta arrived on the Lagos music scene playing this instrument. Adeolu could sing even though he was not endowed with a great singing voice. However, he was a lyrical wizard with great affinity for composing and orchestration. On agidigbo, he was a genius. When he first formed a group called The Rancho Boys, he came to the attention of broadcast media and was featured on the radio. Not long afterwards, the group broke up and he formed another group called Rio Lindo Orchestra. This group consisted of Adeolu (on agidigo and vocals), bongos, maracas, claves, conga drums players, and two chorus singers. A Lagos businessman by the name of Joseph Olajoyegbe Fajimolu with a company under the name of Josy Ola Fajimolu Brothers, who owned a recording company under the label JOFABRO decided to record Adeolu's numbers. When his records were released, Rio Lindo Orchestra with Adeolu not only became extremely popular, agidigbo became popular too. Interestingly enough, popularity of agidigbo music was not in competition with juju music. Adventurous juju musicians decided to experiment with agidigbo and included it in their music. Maracas was also added. Among popular juju artists around this time were Rafiu Bankole, C. A. Balogun, J. O. Araba, J. O. Oyesiku, Theophilus Iwalokun and Suberu Oni.

This decade in which the music should have reached its peak in popularity surprisingly enough, saw its near demise. First of all, lets go back to the 1930s to check its root cause. Nigeria had taken a definitive shape as a country with Lagos as its capital. It was where the action was and everybody wanted to be where the action was. Ethnic groups from different towns of Nigeria were relocating in Lagos. Various types of music were abound and more were still forming. A group of musicians from Calabar in southeastern Nigeria who were mostly horn players formed the Lagos Mozart Orchestra. This band Africanized brass music and had a hit record called *Ore Mi Kini Se* ("My friend why?"... are you running in a hurry). "Steaming" was the name of the group's music. It was popular in marching and parade and it was danceable too, a favorite of the affluents and Lagos elites. Now, this music, after people thought it was long gone, resurfaced in the late 1950s but in another form. Nigerian musicians exposed to Cuban and western style of music overseas and who were now back home after World War II,

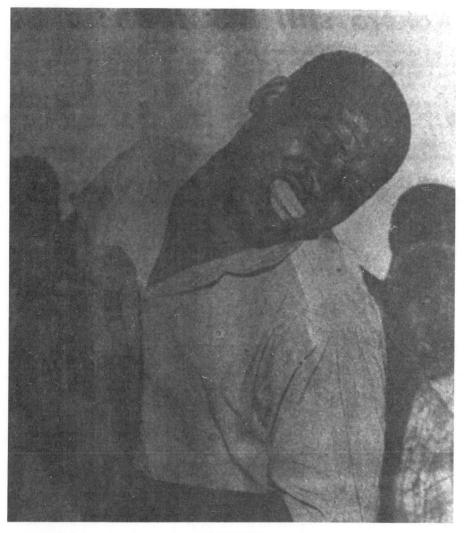

KOKORO

Benjamin Aderonmu Atoneye, the popular Lagos blind tambourine musician popularly known as Kokoro brought Lagos back to juju roots when he surfaced in the nineteen-fifties with his music.

started playing this music. Incorporating guitars and drums in the brass to form a rhythm section, the parade music was revolutionized and called "Highlife" because of its ongoing popularity with the affluents who liked to dance cheek to cheek. The popularity of this music simply drowned juju and sent it into a state of quiescence. Around this time, minstrelsy came back to Lagos with a throwback to the original juju music. A blind man by the nickname of Kokoro (worm/insect) could be seen in the streets of Lagos with the tambourine, starting every of his numbers with the ju-gbu-ju- gbu juju sequence of the original juju music. Since the music had undergone a forty-year drastic change, nostalgia which Kokoro was giving his listeners was actually never really felt. People, by nature, usually show soft spot for any handicap who is trying to eek out a living by earning it and that was why Kokoro soon got to the attention of broadcast media and was featured on radio; but Kokoro wasn't a fluke. He was superb on tambourine. It was amazing what he could do with a one-face drum of seemingly little significance. Born Benjamin Aderonmu Atoneye in Okitipupa in 1921, Kokoro soon showed promise in his school work much to the anger of his jealous father's other wife. The head child of twelve children of his father Prince Atoneye of Owo, Kokoro was having a siesta after school hours one afternoon when this woman poured a mixture of alligator pepper and kolanuts into his eyes. He woke up with a cry of pain and was rushed for treatment but nothing much could be done to retrieve his sight. The following day, the eyes had gone so rotten that a worm was found in one of them (probably hence his nickname of Kokoro). The woman who perpetrated this foul deed was banished from the household after she was rescued from lynch mob. Feeling useless, he left his birthplace, sojourned in few towns and arrived in Lagos in 1947 and later started making a living as a minstrel.

A WHOLE SCENE GOING
THE 1950s
A TUMULTUOUS DECADE

CHAPTER 9
SUB-CHAPTER 9:1

Bobby Benson, Nigeria's granddaddy of highlife music.

MURDER TRIALS •
ALFA APALARA •
ISRAEL NJEMANZE •
HIGHLIFE •

In the courtroom at Tinubu Square Courthouse when he drew a revolver, aimed, fired and killed his best friend Abayomi, for double-crossing him, pandemonium broke loose. When the dust cleared and everybody came out from under the benches, chairs and other various hiding places, he too was found shot in the throat mortally wounded. He had turned the gun at himself too. When Delphonso was rushed to the hospital, the judiciary wanted him healed at all cost by ordering the hospital to give him the best treatment so that he could be properly sent to the gallows. But his mother did something that the Lagosians still remember till today after five decades. She went to Delphonso's hospital bedside and told him that if he dared to survive it, he was a bastard! He didn't survive. Death, that way was preferable to the gallows. He ripped open the sewn up wound and died. It was a deep friendship based on trust that somehow went awry. Lagosians loved valor. Delphonso as far as they were concerned showed one. He was buried with pomp and great ovation. This murder trial in Lagos in the 1920s preceded a tragic one a decade before, of Mrs. Santos who flung a missile that hit her husband on the bridge of the nose and instantly killed him over an argument about the lateness of the lunch that her husband came home to take at lunch-time. However, one of the most memorable juju records was made in the 1940s of a murder trial that shook the whole of Nigeria. Cyprian Tola Oshinnaike, Chief-Clerk of Nigerian Railways was butchered at his house on 32 Little Road, Yaba, on the early morning of Monday 14th October 1946 in connection of which Dickson Nwanko, his Ibo houseboy and Ezekiel Ayodele Kembi, a popular Lagos auctioneer at Idumagbo Avenue, Lagos, were arrested. Magnus Williams a brilliant barrister saved Kembi, who vehemently professed his innocence, from being sent to the gallows. However, in the 1950s, juju musicians had field days with three murder cases and various other events to sing about. Another murder case occurred that again shook the whole of Nigeria. By this time, this particular event in Lagos became memorable because recording in Nigeria had reached an advanced stage as more people had means to afford record discs.

Clearly and simply, Alfa Bisiriyu Apalara was a Moslem preacher who preached the words of Allah, rather than put his beliefs in herbalism, incantations and extra sensory perceptions.

His problem began when he started to preach against the cultists, their profession and religion of paganism. The hardest hit cult was the Oro/Awo-Opa, which supplicated the gods through palm-kernels for childbearing. The turbaned preacher disagreed and claimed that palm-kernel was a seed of the palm-tree and possessed no spiritual or physical power to give child to a woman. He matter-of-factly stated that the only being who possessed the gift of childbearing was the supreme one beyond the clouds whom muslims all over the face of the earth knew as Allah. Not only would the cultists be ran out of business if Apalara was allowed to continue with his assertion, they also stood to lose their respect. And they were very much feared and highly respected. They sent warning to the preacher but he not only ignored it but brazenly gave them a time and date that he would be in their neighborhood, right under their noses to next preach his beliefs. The Oro Cult members decided to do something about him. As the day drew nearer, tension gripped the

Alfa Bisiriyu Apalara

"...the hardest hit cult was the Oro-awoopa secret cult which suplicated the gods through palm-kernel for childbearing. The turbaned preacher disagreed and claimed that palm-kernel is a seed of the palm-tree and possesses no spiritual or physical power to inflate the stomach of a woman with a child." Above, preacher Alfa Bisiriyu Apalara whose problem began when he started to preach against the cultists, their profession and religion of paganism, was killed by the cultist.

"In the ensuing melee, the preacher was grabbed, subdued and hurriedly hauled away to a house to be forever silenced." The house (above) 8 Okobaba Street at Ebutte-Meta on the mainland of Lagos where Alfa Apalara was carried into and believed killed.

Today, located on 8 Okobaba Street is a new building that bears a different number, probably to eliminate the memory of the killing of the preacher. *(picture taken in May 1991)*

air. On a Saturday, at Oko-baba Street in the mainland of Lagos on the night he promised, Apalara with his Koran, two incandescence mantle gas-lamps, and a foot-stool, arrived at an open-air space where he was welcomed by his audience. At first, the embarrassed cultists were nowhere to be seen. Apalara had preached for some time when at exactly 8 o'clock, the whooping sound of the Oro sling filled the air and at the invocation of Oro's name in a shrill and loud voice, the tense atmosphere catapulted into a shemozzle. In the ensuing melee the preacher was grabbed, subdued and hurriedly hauled away to the head of the cultists' house at 8 Okobaba street, Ebute-Metta Lagos. It was believed that after he was killed in the house, heavy stones were tied to his arms and legs and his body was then dumped into the Lagos lagoon right at the back of Okobaba street, to be forever silenced. Few days later when the dust cleared and there was no re-emergence of the preacher, the police was informed and investigation started. The Civil Investigation

Path to the lagoon where Alfa Apalara was drowned.

Division (CID) of Nigeria in Lagos found out that Apalara had been killed, and it started to round up all of the cultists. The headlines in the newspapers were bold and clear. The cultists were wanted. Through series of eliminations, eleven Oro/Alawo-Opa cultists were involved in the extermination of the preacher. His body was never found till today. The trial lasted three months and the whole eleven cultists including Jegede, Omopupa, the Oteka brothers- Raheem and Mustapha, were all sent to the gallows. It was a great day in Lagos. The juju musicians had a field day recording songs about the trial.

One that became a big hit went thus:

Apalara made them to understand
  that the world was beautiful
Apalara made them to understand
  that Oro was nothing but mess.
Only the people involved would be punished
The people involved in conspiring to kill the messenger of God
Only those, would be punished
Say something about this matter in time ye Moslems
All moslems, all moslems, say something about this matter in time.

Lagos lagoon where Alfa Apalara was sunk.

The Yorubas read a lot of meanings to the statements of the line verses of this song but nationally the music was enjoyed greatly.

Not long after this trial, juju itself suffered a big blow. A non-Yoruba musician by the name of Israel Njemanze who played a type of music similar to juju music was murdered by his men and few other accomplices including one named Cyril Anikwe. His decomposed body was found in pieces, dumped near the railway lines at Idi-Oro in the mainland of Lagos. His trial shook the Nigerian music world.

Israel Njemanze
... *"his decomposed body was found in pieces dumped near the railway lines at Idi-Oro in the mainland of Lagos."*
Popular non-Yoruba Lagos musician Israel Njemanze above, who played a type of music similar to juju was murdered by his men and a few other accomplices.

With events like the Queen Elizabeth's and Pope Pius I visits, Marian Congress, The Saint Peter's and Mount Carmel's School building collapse disasters and other events, the Lagos musicians had their hands full in song compositions. But late in the 1950s, something happened. A new music called Highlife arrived on the scene and knocked juju music out of popularity.

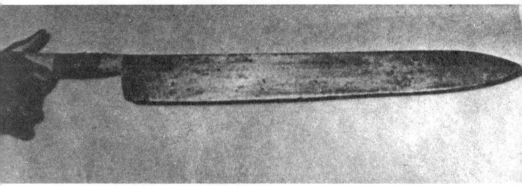

The Big Knife
This is the big knife with which Njemanze's body was cut to pieces and then dumped beside the train lines by his murderers.

During the Njemanze's murder trial, the trial judge, together with some of those charged with the murder were provided with heavy policy guard during a visit to the scene of crime.

HISTORY OF JUJU MUSIC

10

THE 1960s

BOBBY BENSON •
KOBINA CREPY •
HIGHLIFE •
RETURN OF JUJU'S POPULARITY •

In the 1960's, juju bounced back. Before it bounced back however, an antecedent must first be dealt with.

In the 1940s during the World War II, some people, for one reason or another, left the country for overseas. Among them was a young man by the name of Robert Olabinjo Benson. He was an elementary school drop-out because he could not see himself as an academician. Without substantial funds of his own and with a frustrated feeling of worthlessness, he decided to stowaway in a cargo boat; a dangerous but fairly common way of traveling at that time for people that were pecuniary inadequate. His ship was in the Atlantic Ocean when the Luftewaffe mistook it for an enemy ship and bombed it. Before the mistake was realized, the ship was fastly heading down the ocean floor. He was among

Bobby Benson

the people that were saved and put on the Cape Verde Island. There, he met with a lady by the name of *Thunderlio* who taught him how to play the guitar. After some time on the island, he left, continued with his journey and finally arrived in England. There, he learned every musical instrument he could lay his hands on, joined musical troupes and various cabaret groups learning every aspect of stage and show business by sight and instinct. It was during this time that he met his first wife Cassandra, a dancer, who was also dabbling in show-business. He travelled with her to her homeland in the West Indies where he was exposed to Caribbean music and then went on to a host of South American countries to get acquainted with their types of music. Before long, he could play any kind of music including jazz. When the war was over, he decided to come home and formed a cabaret act with his wife with the two billed as CASSANDRA & BOBBY. Robert was ready for Nigeria but Nigeria was not ready for Bobby and so his cabaret act foundered. Frustrated, Cassandra soon left Nigeria for her homeland but Robert was home to stay. If Nigeria was not ready for cabaret, Olabisi knew that music was something the country couldn't do without. Nigeria in particular is a country that exhibits morbid craving for something new so he formed a band called BOBBY BENSON & HIS JAM SESSION ORCHESTRA and brought in a new music with electronic amplification called HIGHLIFE and the whole country went a-gog. But highlife music wasn't new. It was an old brass music of the 1920s with rhythm section now added to it. Other Nigerian musicians from overseas who were back home including Willie Payne, Sammy Akpabot, "Consul" Anifowose and some other local musicians like Tunde Amuwo and Sammy Akpata followed suit and formed highlife bands. Lagos became aglow with social life and cafes and nightclubs were everywhere with live bands.

I. K. Dairo

Young men started to register for music lessons with Kobina Crepy, a music teacher who was a Ghanaian emigrant in Lagos and also with Bobby Benson. Bobby Benson in particular became a trainer for boys who were attracted to musical instruments and flashy attires. At exactly this same time in the neighboring Ghana, highlife music became popular too and Ghana's popular bands included E.T. Mensah and his Tempos Band, Stargazer's Dance

Band of Kumasi, Black Beats, EK's Band, etc. And in London, churning out records that were becoming hits after hits on reaching home in Nigeria were highlife Bands of Ambrose Campbell and His West African Rhythm Brothers, Nat Atkins and His Crazy Bees, Ginger Ishola Folorunso, Rans Boi and Fela Kuti & His Koola Lobitos, etc. In the United States of America, two Nigerians were outstanding--Solomon Ilori and His Drums of Passion and Michael Babatunde Olatunji and His Group. The emergence of highlife music in the late 1950s blitz juju music out of popularity.

Chief Obafemi Awolowo a visionary who lauded I. K. Dairo's award but wished it was of an African or Nigerian origin or creation. Twenty years later, Nigeria created its own honorary awards.

In the 1960s, juju bounced back. The colonial government packed its bag and baggages, lowered the Union Jack and left Nigeria. The country became independent on October 1st, 1960. National awareness ushered in Nigerianization and a craving for something indigenous or down-to-earth set in. Juju music came to the rescue.

A juju music maker by the name of I.K. Dairo adding accordion to his instruments made a record that became a hit. Ordinarily this record would have been just a "run of the mill" but as fate would have it, it became a history making disc. Dairo, an up-country Yoruba, sang in his native dialect adding that touch of Nigerianization. When the record became a hit, it got to the attention of the political establishments. He was nominated for an award and the Nigerian government conferred on him the honorary British title of Member of the British Empire (M.B.E.). (Nigeria was and still is a member of the British Commonwealth). The country went into an uproar and became divided over this award. Some people thought that nothing better could have happened to the African world of music, while some felt that if that award had been given on the first day of the month of April, it would have been a great April Fool's joke while some even went as far as to say that in the absence of April, the Nigerian government must have actually sat down, consumed six kegs of Oguro or Akpeteshi wine, got intoxicated, felt dizzy, flung or fell off its rocker to have awarded a prestigious British honorary title to an African "musician" who could not even read music. Some people even derided the Nigerian Government for being a copy-cat because just exactly around that time, Harold Wilson's Labor government of Great Britain did a similar thing for the British pop group, The Beatles and it caused a great uproar in Britain where people who had received this title for heroism turned in their awards in protest. But some who applauded it included the late Chief Obafemi Awolowo who praised the idea behind the award but felt that it would have been much more laudable if that award had been of an African or better still, Nigerian origin. Whatever the case, the whole affair put life back into juju music and like lightning, many juju groups started sprouting. The music became popular again and worse for highlife music, all the highlife music guitarists that branched to form their own groups formed juju groups instead of highlife bands. Thus highlife music was crushed.

By now, gone were the days of Togo Lawson, Awerende, Denge, and other great pioneers of juju music. By now also, the music had lost its originality and phased out of it were instruments like the tambourine, samba drum, banjo, ukulele, mandoline and agidigbo.

Dele Ojo

Dele Ojo and his Star Brothers Band

Used in playing the music now were electric guitars, sekere, cowbells, gangan (talking drums) bongos, claves, maracas and accordion. Among popular artists around this time were Kayode Ige, Dele Ojo, Tunde Nightingale, I.K. Dairo and down at the end of the line were Ebenezer Obe and Sunny Ade, just up and coming.

Of the decade's most popular artist, none was larger than life and nationwide exceptionally interesting like Dele Ojo.

Dele Ojo became popular on his own. He did not ride on the coat-tails of I.K. Dairo's controversial stardom. He came by way of highlife and brought something new to juju music. Originally a highlife trumpeter, he switched to guitar and injected the highlife style of guitar playing into juju and instead of the usual adamo talking drum of the juju, he surplanted it with Iyalu. Apart from the great co-ordination of his rhythm section, his guitar work was superb.

The first time he came to the public's attention was when he made a record called *I Don't Know Why She Loves Me*. Sung in English, interestingly enough, it was not the wordings, the juju music, nor his beautiful guitar work that made it for him but the heavy and steady beat of the music. After this hit, he pretty soon had a nemesis in the person of Kayode Ige who played exactly his style of music. When the released of his *Enia Bi Aparo* (People like aparo [aparo is a bird]) came out, his adroitness on the guitar showed and left no doubt about his ability as a great instrumentalist and he soon left all his rivals behind. After *Enia bi aparo*, record after record of his was a hit and the airwaves were littered with Dele Ojo's music throughout the country. Chiefs, obas, politicians, everybody who was anybody in the country wanted him for his or her social occasions. The mid 1960s to early 1970s were the rave of overseas tours in which Nigerian bands delighted in for class and eminence. When Roy Chicago and his Abalabi Rhythm Dandies Band, a leading highlife music band went and played in London with resounding success, all the juju groups jumped on the bandwagon and were touring Britain crazily. If a band at that time had not played in London, it didn't have class and amusingly enough, the cover of any LP they made had to bear the picture of when they were boarding the aircraft that took them there with the bold title on the cover reading so so and so band in London.

When Dele Ojo was in London, he caught it by storm. When he first arrived back at home and made a record called *Ilu Oyinbo Dara* (London is good) telling of his experience there during the tour, it was an instant hit. Given the population of Nigeria, if Dele Ojo had had a good manager and a good public relations man, today, he would have been a multi-millionaire and not seek refuge in clergy and become a preacher in a small congregational church in Ibadan to make a living.

With success after success, he undertook so many touring programs and stayed away too long from home. When he first played in Washington D.C. in the USA, the heavens opened. When he arrived back at home, he decided to go back there to stay--a big mistake. He didn't take into account ironies of life and human fickleness. First time appearance rubs newness off anything. The second time around is always welcomed with less enthusiasm --and this was exactly what happened with Dele Ojo. Where actually he failed to take stock of himself was after the USA tour when he released an LP, *Gele Odun* and it bottomed-out in the market. Two young juju artists, up and coming, have stolen the thunder from him, but he failed to take notice and decided to tour again. His next visit to Washington DC was pathetic. Interest over there was lost in him too because he wasn't new anymore and he was eventually reduced to a 9-5 commuter. When he finally came back home, his fans who had not seen him for a while had concentrated on new artists who had brought something new to juju.

Ebenezer Obey who had been with the superb team of Fatayi Rolling Dollar had branched and had been creating waves with the release of some of his singles. When Dele Ojo lost popularity, he (Ebenezer Obey) was the first to come into limelight. He travelled to London on an engagement and when he came back and released his first LP in which he praised all the clubs of various towns of Nigeria that he played for in Britain, his popularity soared. Interestingly enough, his hit number on that LP, *Awa Lomo Abeokuta* (We are Egba indigenes) was a borrowed famous religious tune. In the Easter season of the following year, he released another LP in which the hit tune *Hallelujah* was another borrowed famous religious tune "*Christ the Lord is risen today A-A-A-Alleluujah.*" But the LP that really made it big for him was the one that included the hit tune *Board Members*. This tune was not Obey's original tune either. He borrowed it from an old highlife music record of the late 1950s called AFRICA made by Kwame Nkrumah and the rest of the Stargazers Dancer Band of Kumasi led by Eddie Quansa. The wordings of the record, *Africa, Africa,* etc., etc. were praise song of what Dr. Nkrumah of Ghana did to promote Africa. But Obey made his; *Board members, Board members omo Akerele Board Members tawa ni* --in praise of Akerele and some elite Lagosians who were board members of an establishment. Obey had gone far forward when another juju artist, a guitarist by the name of Sunny Ade who had had a series of unsuccessful singles of name praising discs, came up with a hit song and shook the juju music world.

NOTE: In some sort of a strange way, the Nigerians have a pet aversion for a work which is a version of an original work. To

them, it is copying and people that are involved in such copy work
are called copycats. What in actual fact they dislike is a copy work

Ebenezer Obey

without acknowledgements which makes that work to look as if it's
the original work of the copycat. Because the Nigerian music
industry has a weak copyright infringement law, the copier gets
away without paying for it, takes credit for an unoriginal work if
successful and collects a huge profit if commercialization hit the
product. It was this that embittered 'Tunde Nightingale and which
made him to make a record called *Eyin Oni Copy* (ye Copycats),
tongue-lashing recording artists who prey on the work of others to
gain fame and make money.

Now, the irony of this matter is, to both borrower of a tune (the copycat) and also the original owner of the tune, credits must be given. In the first place, if a tune is not good, it wouldn't worth copying; and it wouldn't be copied, so credit must go to the original owner of the tune. In the second place, if another artist borrows the tune, improves on it, makes his or her version and makes a hit tune out of it, credit must go to the artist because the artist has shown skill and demonstrated sounder reasoning. Now, if this artist is gracious enough to acknowledge the fact that his or hers is a version

Tunde Nightingale

of an original, this would please the Nigerians and that's all they ask.

In the colonial days, one of the most memorable sporting events in Nigeria was the knock-out soccer matches in which the trophy known as the Governor's Cup was a silver cup. The soccer team representing each region of Nigeria vied for this cup in an elimination knock-out match played on a field known as the Association Ground. Later on, the field was renamed King George The V Stadium and finally Lagos Soccer Stadium. After Nigeria's independence from Britain, the cup too was renamed Challenge Cup (see *Challenge Cup* in *A WHOLE SCENE GOING Page 108*).

In 1967 the Challenge Cup match was the hottest ever and Sunny Ade made a record in its memory called *Challenge Cup 1967*. The record became a hit and instantly made him Obey's alter ego. In this decade also, something else happened to juju music. The music which was created and dominated by the Yoruba people soon have a "foreign" artist. An Ibo by the name of Jesus Nwanchuku including accordion in his instruments' and using his native language in combination with pidgin english made a hit record called *Jesus Nwanchuku*, his very name.

In this decade, banjo, ukulele and mandoline were not used in playing the music anymore. Brought in was the accordion. The rest of the instruments were the electric guitars, sekere, cowbells, gangan, conga drums, bongos, claves and maracas.

Fatayi Rolling Dollar

A WHOLE SCENE GOING
THE CHALLENGE CUP

CHAPTER 10
SUB-CHAPTER 10:1

SIR ARTHUR FREDRICHS RICHARD •
U.K. TOURISTS •
"THUNDER" BALOGUN •
"IDI" OMOFEYE •

By the 20th Century, the colonial government had realized that it had overstayed its welcome in Africa and was ready to leave. When it did, there were some established programs that it left behind which the Africans would not compromise. Education, sports, health and a few others were beneficial programs that the Africans would rather improve on and maintain than discard. In sports, the soccer game brought by the British for example became an African staple. In 1945, a soccer competition started in Lagos, with a trophy called, The Governor's Cup, a huge and beautiful silver cup named after the then British governor of Nigeria, Sir Arthur Fredrichs Richard as a winning prize to a victorious soccer team in a knock-out match. The competition was opened to departmental soccer clubs and the very

year it started, it was won by the Nigerian Marine known today as
the Nigerian Ports Authority. It defeated Corinthians by one goal,
the lone goal of the entire match. In 1946, the following year, the
Nigerian Railways beat the cup holder Marine to gain the cup. In
1947, Marine beat Warri in the finals to regain the cup. In 1948 and
1949, Railways beat Port Harcourt twice to regain and retain the cup.

As it usually happens in anything done in groups, there are
individuals that excel. Nigerian soccer had already at this stage

The Challenge Cup silver trophy

had its stars and outstanding players that fans adored and revered.
In Corinthians, Pydoline's days were days when myth and juju
reigned supreme. Earthen pots (oru) containing juju potions could

be seen being carried into the field of play to prevent opponents from scoring.

In the Marine team, goalkeeper Sunny Harte was famous for his dog-sit style of catching ground balls. "Experienced" Ottun was one of the most solid full-back defense players that Nigeria has ever produced. His adroitness in defense work earned him the nickname "Experienced". He was a member of the U.K. Tourists (the team of Nigerian footballers that toured the United Kingdom of Great Britain in 1949). His tragic death after the tour, which ended in suicide when his dead body was found in the Lagos lagoon baffled the whole of Nigeria. Ebenezer "Salamo" the diminutive red-haired left-forward attacker was famous for his nimbleness. His red hair earned him the nickname of "Salamo" (red ant). He too was a member of the U.K. Tourists. There was Hope Lawson, the midfield sweeper, who also played the defence position like a Trojan. And the great E.R.E. Henshaw, center forward and captain of the Marine team who became a legend, with so many mythical stories about him. He and Hope Lawson were members of the U.K. Tourists team too.

In the Nigerian Railways Football Club, (the "Old Reliables") star soccer players swarmed like bees. Badaru was originally the goalie before being replaced by international Ibiam who was a member of the U.K. Tourists. Owundiwe "Agbo" was the resident left-full-back who could head the ball as hard as he could kick it with his foot. This earned him the nickname "Agbo" meaning ram. There was "Idi" Omofeye the right-full-back defense player who later became captain of the team. One snap look at Omofeye and one would dismiss him as an athlete. He was pot-bellied with an over-emphasized buttocks. Actually, his belly was much more protruded than his buttocks, but it was this less exaggerated buttocks that fans seized upon to give him his nick-name "Idi" which simply means buttocks. And Idi, when playing soccer, actually used the buttocks to his advantage as a defense player. With the ball in his possession, he usually blocked his opponents with the pair of the behinds very tightly and firmly so as not to be dispossessed of the ball. When eventually he kicked the ball out of the goal area or the "danger zone", the fans always shouted his nickname "I-di-i-i-i...!!!" reverberating throughout the soccer stadium. And he always looked very pleased. His tragic death was untimely and unexpected. It was ironic that he died exactly on the soccer stadium where he made his name and gained his fame. He was never selected as a member of the U.K. Tourists.

During a soccer match at the King George the V Stadium one hot afternoon, he ran to pick up a ball that crossed over a side line. He had already thrown the ball to one of his teammates when he gently and quietly slumped to the ground. For minutes, he was left unattended to because nobody thought anything was wrong with him. Some even thought he was either clowning or taking a breather. Little did they know that Idi had had a cardiac arrest and had died. It was one of the Cudjoe brothers, Cudjoe Snr., in fact, a teammate and a close friend of his, who started to feel concerned about his lying on the grass without moving and decided to investigate. He was stunned to find Idi lifeless with his eyes rolled up. He frantically waved to the referee to stop the game and Idi was subsequently rushed to the hospital where he was pronounced dead. Cause: Heart attack. His burial was a great and colorful event in Lagos. "Baby" Anieke and P.O. Anosike were great forward attackers who were members of the U.K. Tourists. "Golden Boy" Titus Okere was the neatest player on the field. He was the member of the U.K. Tourists that a British sports reporter referred to as the Nigerian soccer star whose one dribble of his was worth twenty-thousand pounds and a row of houses.

And there was the greatest of them all "Thunder Bolt" Tesilimi Balogun the center-forward who became Nigeria's greatest international soccer star. Tall, a six-footer with bow legs, he was the star whose name conjured magic and whose presence on the field always brought soccer fans in droves to the stadium. A wizard of dribbles, he was the only player at that time who, after the U.K. tour, turned professional and made a successful career out of it. He played for professional clubs in Great Britain and eventually came home in the late 1950's to be the coach of Western Region of Nigeria's soccer team. He died a natural death. In P.W.D. (Public Works Department) there was goalkeeper "Snake" nick-named because of the way he moved but who was later replaced by Dovi and there was Ekunsumi and "I know why" Kolade Williams.

In U.A.C (United Africa Company) there was goalkeeper Thomas, famous for his pair of spectacles which he always wore on the field of play. He was later on replaced by "Gentleman" Carl O'dwyer who, whatever the case might be, was always unruffled on the field of play. There was the great captain Dan Ayam, one of the most handsome players of the time whose great mid-field defense work earned him a position in the U.K. Tourists team. And there was "Small Montana" Sulaimon, a versatile sportsman who was also a boxer and who actually at one time was the Lightweight Champion of Nigeria.

In P&T (Post & Telegraph), there were two soccer stars in Utomi and Achibong and the Police team was known for its skying balls "ayo oke".

Nigerian Railways Team
1956-57 victorious Nigerian Railway soccer team that brought the cup back to Lagos.
Cudjoe Snr. who discovered "Idi" Omofeye's death is seen here holding the cup being carried on the shoulder by his younger brother Cudjoe Jnr. He took on the captaincy of the team after "Idi's" death.

Mention should be made of "Baba" Shittu a great defensive player who was a member of the U.K. Tourists, "Field Marshal " Okosa from the Eastern Region, and Nivasu from the North.

Back to the competition itself, in 1950, UAC defeated Port Harcourt 3-2 to gain the cup. In 1951, the "Old Reliables", The Railways, which probably had won the cup more than any other club, beat Plateau team from Northern Nigeria by 3-2 during extra time. In 1952, Pan Bank beat Warri 6-1. In 1953, Kano beat Dynamos 2-1 at extra time to win the cup. In 1954, Calabar beat Kano 4-1 to win the cup. In 1955, Port Harcourt won the cup. In 1956 and 1957 the "Old Reliables" were at it again. The Railways beat Warri 3-1 and Zaria 5-0 respectively to bring the cup back to Lagos and to retain it in Lagos the succeeding year. In 1958, Port Harcourt beat Federal United 6-0 to win the cup. In 1959, Ibadan beat Police 2-1 to take the cup to Western Nigeria. In 1960 the ECN (Electricity Corporation of Nigeria) won the cup and brought it back to Lagos.

When soccer first started in Nigeria, the organizers formed a club known as the Nigerian Football Association (NFA). The field at the Victoria Island acquired for playing matches was then known as Association Ground. Later, its name was changed to King George the V Stadium in honor of the King of England. After Nigeria's independence from Great Britain, the name was changed to Lagos Stadium. The cup's name changed too from the Governors Cup to the F.A. Cup and finally the Challenge Cup. Soccer matches in Nigeria has always been hot but probably the hottest so far was the 1967 one which Sunny Ade made a record of. It was this record that brought him fame.

A WHOLE SCENE GOING
POST-WAR LAGOS

STAGE PLAYS •
HUBERT OGUNDE •
LAYENI •
G.T. ONIMOLE •

When Bobby Benson returned home to Lagos after the World War II, he came with a cabaret act in a team with his wife Cassandra. Their act never took off the ground. It wasn't that Nigeria was not ready for stage plays, it was just that for some strange reasons they just couldn't pull it off despite the glitter and the fast moving pace that accompanied their act. As a matter of fact, stage work had existed in Nigeria ever since music was around. Prominent in commercially oriented stage plays were dramatists like Hubert Ogunde, Layeni, G.T. Onimole among others. Far in front and away from all others in a long stretch was Hubert Ogunde, a Yoruba, who by nature was a dramatist. He perfected his art with visits to Britain. A polygamist, he involved his wives in his work and taught them how to play saxophones. The head-wife whom he took with him overseas became his principal dancer and she was featured prominently in all of his plays. Ninety percent of his plays were biblical and churches throughout Nigeria always hired him to stage biblical plays for them. It wasn't until the late 1950s when he hit it with a non-biblical play called *HIGHWAY EAGLE* that he started getting the recognition due to him. In the early 1960s, a turn-about came to him. He formed a recording company and started making recordings on his own label. Not only that, he started to record other musicians as well on his label. With his troupe which included his wives and young strong men who were energetically rich in dramatics, ironically he didn't personally get nationwide attention until when in the early 1960s he made a controversial record called *Yoruba Ronu* (Yoruba, think) in which he cautioned the Yorubas not to be reduced to a state of impotence into which they were fast degenerating. The record didn't sit down too well with some Yoruba political leaders and was consequently banned in some few places. The uproar over this, catapulted him into national prominence. A saxophonist himself, he has a rich and good singing voice. Endowed with a high sense of composing, every one of his musical compositions carried a message. Ethnically rigid, Ogunde was one of the few Yorubas that adhered to "Ijinle Yoruba" (in-ground or deep Yoruba) which unequivocally showed in every aspect of his thought, word and deed.

May be for the sake of progress every star needs a rival and this was where Layeni came in, pitched against Ogunde; but in theatrical quality was no match for the veteran. Ubiquitous and approachable, Layeni revelled in merriments. When not on stage, he could be seen rendering his musical services in parades and carnivals flashing his white teeth and rolling his big eyes. His stage plays varied from biblicals to musicals. In the late 1950s when he became a hotelier, there was a need for him to have a band so he formed Layeni and His Syncopation Orchestra. Exceptionally jolly, his two favorite instruments were the trumpet and saxophone. G.T. Onimole was of a different stuff. A lyrical wizard, song composition was his forte. His stage work was around exactly at the time that Layeni and Ogunde were vying for leadership but he stayed away from the struggle concentrating more on folk stories for stage work which was sporadic. He was better known as song composer for churches and communities in need of praise songs for harvest and thanksgiving services. A guitarist by trade, rhythm and melody came to him naturally. He could sing very well too.

When Benson arrived from England, his stage plays were not in any competition against these men. His, was different and much more westernized. Problem was, he never turned people on.

None of these activities ever constituted any threat to juju music which at this time was in its fifth decade and growing in popularity. As a matter of fact, juju was borrowing from them to improve itself.

11

THE 1970s—A DECADE OF TWO RIVALS

EBENEZER OBEY •
SUNNY ADE •
MILITARY REGIME •
ACQUISITION OF FICTIVE TITLES •

By the 1970s, juju music had left no doubts as to the fact that it was the music that the public was much sought after. Juju musicians were fiercely and constantly experimenting with various musical instruments to make sure that dominance of its influence on the public did not falter. Immediately Sunny Ade got off the ground with his disc "Challenge Cup 1967", there was no stopping him anymore and with each LP record made, he was gathering fans along the way. Obey didn't take to the hills but he knew a rivalry was in the making. Every star had his nemesis. Bobby Benson had Sammy Akpabot, Victor Olaiya had Chief Bill Friday, Roy Chicago had Eddie Okonta, Dele Ojo had Kayode Ige, Fela Kuti had Orlando Julius, etc. etc., so Lagos just braced up itself for two good artists who were ready to deliver the goods. As things usually turn out, the artists weren't the elements that make enemies of each other but their fans who always concoct vicious rumors to juice-up things and fan hatred. As Sunny Ade was getting more popular, Ebenezer Obey too was making waves and rumor started to circulate that the two of them disliked each other and were clearly on war-path. The two central characters knew that they did not dislike each other and Sunny Ade, to dispel that rumor, went on Thursday the 16th of August, 1973, to Obey's night spot called Obey Miliki Spot and enthusiastically joined Obey on the bandstand to knock-off some tunes on the guitar to the relief and wild approval of music loving Lagosians who would rather hear the two make good music than fight. Not only that, he included in his VOL II LP released at the time, a number called *Oro to nlo* in which he chastised the fans on both sides to stop tattle-taling and causing problems that were unnecessary.

By now, gone were the days of Ebenezer Obey's single hits like *Ara mi ese pelepele* and others that were household favorites. He has improved his music and he was matured greatly as a man. On the other side, Sunny Ade subconsciously was nearing some milestones in juju music. He introduced organ which really didn't catch on and discarded it but to re-introduce it a few years later with success. Together with Chief Atolagbe, he introduced drum set in juju music.

In the mid-sixties when the Nigerian military took over the government of the country, the take-over in some ways had some effects on juju music. One of them could clearly be reflected in name changing tinged with a taste of power by some musicians. An example was Obey who did not want to be known simply as Ebenezer Obey anymore; he has put a title with quotes before his name. With his name now read "Chief Commander" Ebenezer Obey, this was mildly diverting since Mr. Fabiyi would rather see people dance to his music than snap to A-tten-shun! Further with the incongruities, heavens only knew the reason for the letter "y" in front of the name he chose for his last. Would Obe have sounded terrible than Obey? Or wouldn't the Yoruba accent on the "e" (Obe) have made his name sounded as in the English word Obey as he would have liked it pronounced? Would the fictive title of Chief Commander have made his authority less obeyed until his name was spelled with a "y"? The Yorubas certainly do spell their Obe without a "y" and Obe without a "y" is more African and more beautiful. And lastly, did he even comprehend the implication of his band's new name, The Inter Reformers Band? If he had sought for advice, he never would have called the boys reformers. None of his boys has ever been

RIVALS
Ebenezer Obey (left) and Sunny Ade

reformed or been in a reformatory or was there any? Did he know that reformers are like ex-prisoners?

Anyway as a music maker, Ebenezer is good. Non-Nigerians who have heard his music even pointed out in no uncertain terms that his music was the best of all the current crop of juju musicians.

In the 1970s, sekere and accordion were rarely used in the playing of juju music but the number of the players have increased. A juju band at this time variously numbered fourteen to fifteen players.

HISTORY OF JUJU MUSIC

12

THE 1980s

JUJU MUSIC CAME
TO INTERNATIONAL PROMINENCE

FELA KUTI •
SUNNY ADE •
SLIDE GUITAR •
SIDE SHOWS •
BIG BAND SIZE •
ANOTHER MILESTONE •

Africa is a continent. There are forty-six countries in the continent of Africa. Each African country has its division of countless ethnic groups and tribes which have their various types of music; so one can imagine how many different types of music are in Africa. In West Africa, the most popular music is the highlife music because of its western influence yet internationally it is not popular. Before now, big name labels and world renown recording companies were not interested in promoting African music except ethnic or tribal music that they wanted to use for special purposes like documentaries, films or radio broadcast in order to make or emphasize a point. Like calypso, jazz, classical, rock and pop music that are known and enjoyed internationally, no African music has attained this stature or privilege. The world established recording companies which should be responsible for this simply came, pitch-forked their plants in these various African countries, started recording local artists for local consumption and ferried the revenues out of the countries. To them, the African musics however good, were not good enough for international recognition and fame. But that started to change from the late 1970s upwards. It is true that African records and musics can be found in any overseas countries' record stores but these are in limited quantities perhaps purposely for diplomats craving for things homespun or for educational purposes in learning institutions.

Great and talented African artists, some, who even received their music education in established and world renown music colleges ached in their hearts about the selfishness and neglect of these recording companies which would rather promote anything but African music because the African music however good, was not their idea of commercial music and putting their efforts in its promotion were to them a sheer waste of time.

Perhaps the shape of things to come took its root in the music of a young Nigerian by the name of Fela Kuti in the late 1960s. During his music studies in Great Britain in the late 1950s, he became familiar with a lot of western type of music including rock, jazz, soul and pop. When he returned home in the early 1960s, he dabbled in highlife music which he was familiar with, for a while, but he did not make any headway. He then invented his own music by mixing African music with rock in an explosion of heavy African drumming. He called it AFROBEAT. It was so complex that few people could analyze the music that he was trying to play. Pot and crack shots were taken at him but he was neither riled nor daunted. The more crack shots were taken at him, the more he persisted and his persistence bordered on craziness. A few people bought his singles because the majority thought they were abominations but he persisted. They called him a freak, a nut, and a lunatic fringe, but still, he persisted. They said that he lacked the ability to compose a song fully and that his music was noisy, heavy, and hard to decipher but he persisted. When his first LP which included a collection of some of his singles was released, only two-hundred and fifty were sold and that was after they stayed on the rack at the E.M.I. warehouse in Apapa for a long time; nobody touched them. Mr. Wells, the managing director at E.M.I. studios at Apapa at that time was so dismayed, he had to reduce at give-away prices these LP's before he could rid of the two-hundred and fifty lot. But this young man could not care less nor back off.

When the LP reached England, Mrs. Cecil Gee at Stern Radio Record Stores at London's Warren Street took in a few. Two days

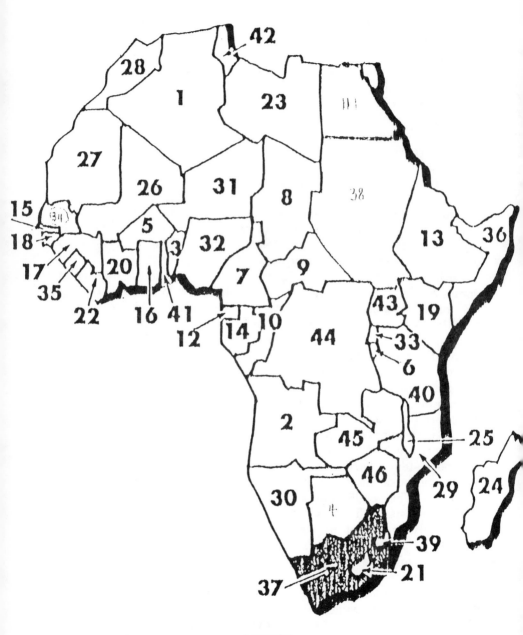

AFRICA
Africa is a continent comprising of 46 countries.

Tribal map of Africa
This is how Africa would have looked liked if it is based on tribe.

Fela Kuti

after stocking these few, she went absolutely crazy. Ranting, raving and throwing temper tantrums at the supplier, she commanded that the records be removed from her stores because she had never in her entire sales life seen a merchandise this much spurned by Africans and most especially Nigerian record buyers. But Fela ceded not one inch. He was dogged because of the belief that he had in himself and in time, he started to get recognition. Also he was improving. Then by the late 1960s, he did one thing; he employed a lady dancer and created a side show. Also, when he refused to leave the scene, people by now were starting to accept him and in 1969, he took his act overseas. The complexity of his music was the first thing to catch the attention of western listeners and observers and from then on the gate was slit-open for the international recognition of African music. Today, nobody has to be told about Fela's gigantic musical success because everybody knows.

Now came in Sunny Ade. Whether it was Fela's example he followed still remained debated but on the same line of Fela Kuti, he gathered some dancing girls, garbed them in mini-skirts made of African materials which were sequined with cowries, and supplied them with fly-whisks to aid them in dancing. It worked but he soon discarded the girls to replace them with men dancers who doubled as chorus singers. When he brought his act overseas, a French and an American theatrical agents discovered that his act was concert-like and that college students could easily relate to it and to him as an individual. Then started massive publicity never before seen in African music. Instantly, Sunny Ade lost his dancing clients because these theatrical agents did not think the way the Africans think. They were more commercial oriented and they have plans for their newly found artist. European and American tours were booked for Sunny Ade and publicity was at its highest.

When Sunny Ade invaded Europe, it was the size of the band that first made the audience flip. Then the drumbeat, most especially the talking drummers and lastly the call and response type of singing. The sideshow dancing, though not particularly great was appreciated too. Since the European invasion was a success, advanced forays into the United States of America put music enthusiasts in a state of anticipation. When the king came to America to play in a concert, he was a huge success more than that of Europe. However, Sunny has twice been in the U.S. before the 1970s to play for the Nigerian students and their friends, but never on a huge promotional scale like this. This time, everybody knew what juju music was all about. By bringing juju Music to international prominence, Sunny Ade brought it to another milestone.

Fela Kuti's first LP record released in the late 1960s, for a long time, record buyers did not want it.

AFRICAN TOURS

PRESENTS

AGAIN IN NEW YORK CITY
AFRICA'S MOST SOULFUL BAND

FELA RANSOME - KUTI

AND HIS

KOOLA LOBITOS

TOURING FROM WEST AFRICA

at the HOTEL DIPLOMAT
108 West 43rd St. between 6th Ave. & Broadway

Friday, July 11, 1969
From 9 p.m. to 3 a.m.

ALSO FEATURING: Exotic Afro Beat demonstrator,
MISS DELE JOHNSON

MASTER OF CEREMONIES: DAPO ODEBIYI

Tickets: $3.50

For Tickets, Reservations and further information, contact:

Ajayi Martins 622-2934	Lanre Adebisi 858-8071
Jimmie Asolo 638-4197	Yinka Johnson 857-9831
Hamid Abiola 857-0755	Charles Fadipe 443-7900

"*Afro beat is pure soul coming from soul's original home*" · WOOK-TV WASH. D.C.
"*This is something new, sweet and very African*" · OBSERVER

Handbill of Fela Kuti's tour of 1969 which probably opened the door
of recognition for African music internationally.

MILESTONES
'TUNDE KING
(Alhaji Abudurafiu Babatunde King)
† THE NAMING OF JUJU MUSIC
† THE NAME "JUJU" ON RECORD DISC LABEL
† ESTABLISHMENT OF CERTAIN NUMBER OF
  MUSICIANS IN A GROUP

Tunde King, the old king of juju music, generally credited as the founder of the music was the first artist to reach the first three milestones in juju music.

Born in 1910 at 33 Bishop Street, in the then Saro congregated Okearin neighborhood of Lagos, ten years after the music was started by the Lagos minstrels without any particular name to it, his contributions to the music made it what it is today.

He attended Olowogbowo Primary School and Western Olowogbowo Boy's High School, Lagos. During his school days, he met a friend by the name of Ariyo who was a student of the C.M.S. Grammar School and who knew how to play the guitar very well. He joined and learned a lot about guitar playing from this young man and pretty soon the two of them were playing for the crewmen from ships that arrived from overseas.

After his association with the music for a period of time, he decided to form his own group around 1932, which consisted of four men including a samba drum player. To give his music the feeling of the new and popular tambourine music that was attracting public attention at the time, he went to the Salvation Army stores, bought a tambourine and gave it to his samba drummer. The samba drummer developed a style of tossing the tambourine up in the air and catching it much to the delight of the dancers, onlookers or listeners. The Yoruba word for toss or throw is "ju". Duplicated with tonal accent, it becomes juju. The onlookers applied this to the action of the samba drummer and in time to the music itself. Thus, twenty-eight years after the music surfaced on the Lagos scene, it eventually had a name to it thereby reaching its first milestone.

In 1936, four years after juju music was christened, 'Tunde King made some recordings on Parlophone label. He was the first artist to have the name of his music put on this label as "JUJU" and so the second milestone in juju music was reached.

After the release of his records on Parlophone label in 1936, other juju music groups started to copy the format of his group which became standard for a long time and so juju music reached a third milestone. 'Tunde's group consisted of four musicians--he, the leader, on six-stringed guitar-banjo and vocals, Ishola Caxton-Martins on sekere (gourd rattle), Lamidi George on tambourine (juju), Sanya Johnson on symbols or tom-tom and later on Ejo (Snake) on gangan. These players all supplied harmony as 'Tunde led on vocals and guitar.

Tunde King

His first record *Eko Akete* was made in 1936 and after that he made many more others including *Sapara ti lo s'ajule orun, Oba Oyinbo, Dunia (Amuda), Ojo nla lojo agan* etc, etc. In all, he made over 30 records.

When the World War II broke out in 1939, he left music and Lagos altogether and took a job on a ship as a greaser, applying grease to the ship's engine for smooth running and proper maintenance; and off he went to England. When the war was over, he came back to Nigeria in 1945 to pick up where he left off. By this time, other juju artists that had sprang up and copied his style included Akanbi Ege, Ayinde Bakare, Ojoge Daniel and Tunde Nightingale.

The sage, who saw the earliest part of colonial rule in Nigeria is the most authoritative informant on juju and other Nigerian types of music. Three quarters of his entire life which was devoted to juju music was interwoven with many of his compositions which typified the life in the "good old days" of Lagos in its formative stage. The tumultuous reign of Oba Esugbayi Eleko and his several problems with the colonial government (1900-1932), The World Wars I & II (1932-1945), The death of Herbert Macaulay, The Missionaries, the various religious groups and their performances etc., etc.

Tunde's music could be fast and danceable but in most cases, it is slow and easy going. And of all the milestones reached in juju music, his first three milestones were the three most significant in juju music.

Tunde King is a proud grandfather. He has three daughters of his own. In 1983, he went on a Hadji pilgrimage to Mecca which made him an Alhaji on his return to Nigeria. Today, he lives peacefully in Isheri on the outskirts of Lagos, retired but not tired.

NOTE: The following is another account of the naming of juju music given by Tunde King on June 3, 1991 in a video interview years after he had made the above and aforewritten statements. This account should not be taken as a contradiction but an addition to the various accounts of the naming of the juju music.

"When I formed my own group in 1932, I had to send somebody to buy me a tambourine at the Salvation Army Store because they wouldn't sell it to any ordinary person. I played for important people in Lagos like lawyers, doctors, engineers, politicians and so on but mostly for doctors. I had a doctor friend in the person of Dr. Oguntola Sapara, the famous Massey Street Dispensary medical practitioner who always called me to play for him in any of his social big-dos. Consequently all of the doctor friends of Oguntola Sapara started to use my band for their social engagements and so I became their personal or resident band. In Lagos at that time, the doctors were called *"Onisegun" and affectionately referred to as "juju" men,"ogun" meaning juju. Because I was the musician who always played for the juju men, they called my music juju

music. But this did not happen until Tuesday 4th of June, 1935, when Dr. Oguntola Sapara died and I was called to play at his "awakening" and funeral.

That was a day to behold. All of the juju men (doctors) of Nigeria were there and lawyers, architects, engineers, politicians and so on were there too. I composed a song for Dr. Sapara called "Sapara ti lo si ajule orun" (and later recorded it) and when I played it on that day, Pandemonium broke loose and they called my music juju music meaning the music of the "Oniseguns" (the music of the doctors).

*Incidentally, the actual meaning of doctor in Yoruba is Oniwosan (the person who treats ailments) and not Onisegun (the person who makes medicine). Onisegun in english means pharmacist. The inagos of Lagos mistakenly gave the wrong name to a right profession.

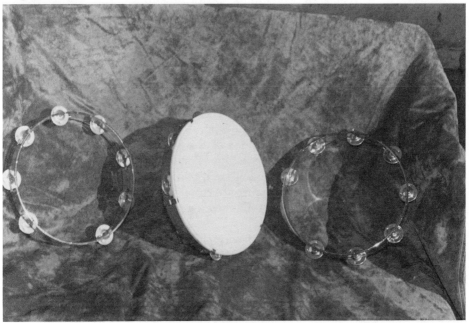

Tambourines

MILESTONES
AKANBI WRIGHT
(*Akanbi Ege*)

† ARGUABLY, FIRST TO USE TALKING DRUM IN JUJU MUSIC

† FIRST JUJU MUSICIAN WHOSE COMPOSITION WAS ADOPTED AND SUNG BY SCHOOL CHILDREN ALL OVER NIGERIA IN FORM OF AN ANTHEM.

One of the young and brilliant minds in juju music who performed in Lagos spanning a two decade period of 1930s-1950s was Akanbi Ege.

Born in Lagos of the repatriates parentage, his ability to use well thought out lyrics in his music actually gained juju music the miniscule of respect that it had at the time. By the time that he fully immersed himself in juju music, he had espoused the ideas of the nationalistic movement championed by Herbert Macaulay, the great Nigerian politician and defender of the native rights, and had become political.

Since life in Lagos around this time was somehow full of politics, Akanbi's stock rose with every record that he made and his popularity was nearly at parity with Tunde King's, the period's king of juju music who was leader of the juju group that the Lagos elites solely patronized. Before the World War II, his popularity had peaked and he had boasted of such geniuses like J.O. Araba and others as members of his band. (Araba was to later form a juju group that played a popular type of music which was an off-shoot of juju, called "Toy Motion.")

World War II in some sort of way shifted Akanbi Ege from small scale city to national scale attention. The war had affected the nation of Nigeria by bringing personal and day-to-day inconveniences to the Nigerians. Food was controlled by rationing, young men were being sent to the fronts of Burma and North Africa. The country was constantly threatened by Erwin Rommel's offensives in Egypt and Libya in Africa northward of Nigeria.

In support of Britain and the other countries which were against Hitler, Akanbi Ege made a record that went thus:

Hitiler ti nda aiye ru o
(Hitler, who is throwing the world into confusion)
E f agara ti si koto o
(Use shovel to push him in the grave)

Given the reputation of juju music at that time, it hardly would have been a record suitable for acceptance in learning institutions but Akanbi Ege deviated from juju music and played the tune in "native-air" style. It became a big hit and was nationally song in schools to show support for the colonial government in Nigeria which was administering the British rule in the country; a rarity and a first of its kind. He also made some other records on World War II including *The Five Nigerian R.A.F.*

After the war, Akanbi Ege increased the instrumentation of his music with a talking drum in 1948. He was said to be the first person to introduce this drum in juju music but some juju observers had argued that gangan drums had been played in juju music well before World War II. Akanbi Ege never lasted as some people would have wanted. The root of what caused his demise could be traced back to the 1920s.

Herbert Macaulay formed a political party, The Nigerian National Democratic Party (NNDP) in 1923. By the 1930s, Akanbi Ege was one of the young men caught in the wave of this nationalistic movement of Macaulay and he had changed his name from Akanbi Wright to Akanbi Ege and supported the NNDP. In 1946, Macaulay was ailing very badly and his right-hand man, a young Nigerian intellectual by the name of Nnamdi Azikiwe, an Ibo by tribe, had formed a new political party, The National Council of Nigeria and the Cameroons (NCNC) and had asked the ailing old man to be its first president and with him as the Vice President. Macaulay had accepted. The NNDP then coalesced with the NCNC to become one. Around this time, another young man who had espoused the ideas of Herbert Macaulay and who was living far and away from Nigeria, found the move of Nnamdi Azikiwe a treachery because the NCNC, to him, was Ibo tribe dominated. This man by the name of Obafemi Oyeniyi Awolowo, then studying Law and Economics in London invoked the name of Oduduwa, the founder of the Nigerian Yoruba tribal people and formed a cultural party using his (Oduduwa's) name and urged all Yorubas to join the party called Egbe Omo Oduduwa (The Party of Oduduwa Children).

A lot of Yorubas joined this cultural group but those that refused to join included Akanbi Ege. He remained with the NNDP.

Meanwhile the NNDP-NCNC were known as the "Demo" (short for democracy), and the political problem of the time centered around land acquisition by the colonial government. National tours were scheduled in which Macaulay was to make speeches to assure the Nigerians that their lands would not be taken from them *(see SEIGNEURIAL RIGHT, ETC. in SPECIAL MENTION on Page 155)* but it was at the beginning of this tour that Macaulay started to ail badly and had to be returned home.   Not long afterwards on May 7, 1946, his life ebbed away. The NNDP was then fully incorporated in NCNC under one name and Dr. Nnamdi Azikiwe became President of the party.

When Awolowo later arrived back in Nigeria, he formed a political party known as the Action Group (AG) and brought into it the Egbe Omo Oduduwa.   He formed this party in the Yoruba heartland of Ibadan in the Western region of Nigeria.

Because the Western Nigeria election was in the offing and because he needed more base to operate, he theorized that Lagos founded by the Yorubas of Nigeria belonged to the Western region of Nigeria and sought to incorporate it in the West.   The Demo, the major opponent of the AG begged to differ thereby causing a big conflict between the two parties.   This was in the 1950s.   Now, Akanbi Ege, a supporter of the NCNC which was also known as the Demo, went and made a record called *Demo lo l'Eko* (Demo is the owner of Lagos) which became a big hit. That was just about the last of this brilliant musician. This record did him in. Akanbi Ege, not long after the success of this record, was afflicted with a terrible disease that crippled him. He suffered for a long time before death took him out of his misery. It was rumored that those who did not like his support of the Demo, cast a bad magical spell on him for punishment.

MILESTONES
THEOPHILUS IWALOKUN
† DEBATABLY, FIRST TO SING JUJU SONG IN
NATIVE DIALECT

In the early part of the 1960s, a plum young African American in the United States of America by the music name of Chubby Checker invented a dance called the Twist. This dance became famous world-wide and the popularity of it made an impression that raised the black race's pride.

It was thought that it would be a permanent fixture on the wall of dance but a few years after its invention, Twist was blown off the scene. The replacement of the dance's excitement came in another form and from the other side of the Atlantic of America. In Liverpool, England, four young men in a group called the Beatles caused sensation throughout the world with their music and made a lasting impression that raised a nation's pride. For this, they were rewarded with British honorary titles. This was in the middle of the 1960s. Just exactly around this time, a similar thing was happening in Nigeria. Nationalism was the attention apprehenser. Caught in the wake of this nationalistic movement, a Nigerian juju music player called I.K. Dairo, made a record, singing in his native dialect. This record became a big hit and he too was rewarded with a British honorary title of M.B.E. (Member of the British Empire).

However, I.K. Dairo was not the first juju musician to sing in his native dialect. His supposedly innovation was a question of being in "the right place at the right time" because it was said that thirty years before, a juju music player by the name of Theophilus Iwalokun who hailed from Ibereke, a province of Okitipupa had sung or had always been singing his music in his native dialect. Some other artists in this wise were mentioned also.

Theophilus Iwalokun was one of the early players of juju music. He started in the 1930s when juju music took off in Lagos. His early recordings could bear testimony to the assertion of the people who were in the know.

MILESTONES
AYINDE BAKARE
(RIP)
† FIRST TO USE MICROPHONE –1949

One of the most respected and loved Nigerian juju musician was Ayinde Bakare.

Born in the Lafiaji neighborhood of Lagos of Yoruba parents, he was "Mr. juju music" because throughout his entire life, he lived juju music. Every single of his recording reflected the sound and spirit of juju music, juju music as it should be played-- unadulterated, meaningful and satisfying. Of all juju artists, he was the only one who had undiluted and enormous passion for women. He made records that were hits after hits singing praises of their beauty and behavior *Iwa Lewa*, prayed for pregnant women *Adura Fun Awon Aboyun,* gave pieces of advice to the newly-weds, and warned women on jealousy *Ojowu Obinrin*, entreated young women never to commit abortion, etc., etc.

An early player of the music, he never borrowed a tune, copied or played the lyrics of other artists. He was original through and through. He was never out of popularity and was never unwanted. All of the lyrics of his compositions were meaningful and purposeful. A list cannot be made of his admirers and fans.

In the early 1930s at the early stages of his music career, the number of players in his group was what he maintained throughout his playing days because to him juju must not be compromised in any shape or form.

When the World War II was over in 1945, advancement in electronics hit Nigeria's world of music. Megaphone was discarded and electronic amplification took over. Ayinde Bakare was on Ukulele-banjo when he was to try the microphone as a booster. The small size of his Ukulele-banjo could have prevented this from happening so he decided to play the guitar which had a bigger surface area instead and which could accommodate the pick-up. The available pick-up was the contact microphone so he attached this to the guitar and thenceforth became a guitarist but little did he know that he had made history because he became the first juju musician to use microphone. Thus another milestone was reached in juju music.

By the 1950s, he had become so well-known that his popularity stretched beyond Nigeria, his native country, to overseas. Social demand made him to finally undertake a Great Britain tour in 1957 where he performed in so many historical town halls and also met the great Ambrose Campbell and in particular Ade Bashorun who was the great force in bringing him to the attention of Melodisc Records which recorded one of his best and most memorable albums which today is a collectors item.

Even though he himself was a guitarist and the lead singer of his band, yet the emphasis he placed on the Nigerian talking drum made the drum synonymous to juju music.

When he didn't sing about women, then philosophy, name praising etc. were his secondary pets. He never forgot a good thing done to him and an event either good or bad would never pass without Ayinde Bakare making a record in memory of it. During the Nigerian Independence, in 1960, his engagements were many and he fulfilled every one of them without splitting his group.

Jazz artists, highlife music makers and all the people in entertainment business, have a certain kind of fondness and respect for Mr. Ayinde Bakare. But could the man who had made many people happy and brought joys to the homes of millions of people through his music had a suppressed undercurrent problem that was desperately searching for an escape? If not, what then could have made Ayinde Bakare to die the way he died? Did Ayinde Bakare commit suicide? If not, did the very sect of people he felt strongly about did him in? Late in his life when everybody thought he was still enjoying his work, he was at an engagement when during the half-time he told his boys that he would like to tend to something and that he would be back in a minute. He never came back.

According to sources closely associated with his last hours, about two women came around and invited him to come along with them for either a tryst or jollity somewhere separately and away from his social engagement. It was an offer too good to be refused and he left with the women.

When his boys didn't see him return, they entered the second-half without him hoping he would join them soon. He never did. When playing was over, the now worried boys all departed to their homes more worried. Some days later his dead body was found in the Lagos lagoon. What a shock the sad event gave to the whole nation. He never left a suicide note. And if he didn't, he possibly didn't commit suicide. Now, if Ayinde Bakare seemed not to have committed suicide, why wasn't there a probe on his mysterious death? Why wasn't anybody, any single body, demand an investigation to his death? Who were the two (or whatever number) women who came around to take him away from his engagement during the half-time? Where did they take him to? For what? And to do what? Who was the person who engaged him to play for this particular social occasion? Shouldn't these questions be asked?

Ayinde Bakare

Ayinde Bakare in London

Mr. Bakare   left an indelible mark on the surface of Nigerian music but if he felt that it was fitting for his soul to rest in a cold, peaceful and liquid medium, then may his soul rest in peace.

MILESTONES
I.K. DAIRO
(Isaiah Kehinde Dairo)
† FIRST TO RECEIVE AN HONORARY TITLE M.B.E. (MEMBER OF THE BRITISH EMPIRE) FOR JUJU MUSIC AND FOR MUSIC IN GENERAL

Because of the morbid craving that the Nigerians usually exhibit for anything that is western or western influenced, the highlife music which is heavily straddled with western musical instruments when it arrived on the Nigerian scene in the 1950s, was thought to have carved a permanent place for itself in the social life of the Nigerians.

Less than three years after the Nigerian independence from Great Britain in 1960, surprisingly, it had totally burnt itself out.

In the early 1950s, a tough-minded and an extremely nationalistic Ibo politician by the name of Mazi Nbonu Ojike dubbed "Mr. Boycott," had urged the Nigerians to boycott anything western starting from the day-to-day attire which the colonial government has condemned as ill-fitting and not smart enough for the office. Later another equally nationalistic Nigerian Yoruba politician, Chief Obafemi Awolowo has taken up the cry of Ojike and has advocated for Nigerianization and Africanization. After independence, the self awareness came and the highlife music was one of its victims.

Highlife music was not good anymore and the nation was looking for something indigenous, something down-to-earth. A juju musician by the name of Isaiah Kehinde Dairo who later became popular as I.K. Dairo decided to bring accordion into juju music. But accordion!? Yes, accordion. Well, wait-a-minute, accordion is not an African made musical instrument, is it? No, it's not but the instrument played an accessory part of which brought juju music to another milestone. Even though Nigeria was looking for something more homely, it was Mr. Dairo's dialect together with the use of accordion which brought him into the limelight.

Dairo is from the country-side with a heavy accent and an intonation which the Lagosians found diverting. Making a record with a combination of these together with an accordion plus heavy drumming, gave the nation what it was looking for. In one stroke, Dairo became popular. His music somehow came to the attention of politicians. What followed was a controversy that the nation didn't bargain for. For popularizing a Nigerian indigenous music, he was awarded the British honorary title of M.B.E. (Member of the British Empire).

Opinion immediately became divided over this award. Those for it, maintained that nothing better could have happened to Nigerian music. Those against it were even more divided. Some said that there were more indigenous types of music around whose players should have received the award while some complained that Nigeria was still wallowing in colonial mentality by awarding to a Nigerian, a British honorary title. But what these people have forgotten was that Nigeria was and is still a member of the British Commonwealth. Because some Nigerians have been tuned to believe that honorary titles, except in academic instances, are awarded for valor, some of the cons took the whole thing as a joke and even jested that the Nigerian government, when it was in the process of making the award, was in the throes of hallucination. But for whatever it was worth, the award stuck and juju groups started sprouting.

In the 1960s and early 1970s, he made a tour of overseas countries where he played for the Nigerian communities in Great Britain and some other parts of the United Kingdom.

He is known as "Baba Aladura" because of his many compositions that are prayer oriented, and he once changed the name of his brand of juju music to "Ashiko" music. In addition to accordion, he also plays the guitar and the talking drum.

I.K. Dairo was born in 1930 in Offa at the time that his father was in the employ of the Nigerian Railway Corporation. His parents actually hailed from Ijebu-Ijesha where they finally settled. When early in his life he showed interest in music, he was greatly encouraged. Music must be running in his family blood because his younger brother is the famous "Mr. Topless," the skilled saxophonist Orlando Julius, leader of the defunct Modern Aces Band. As a matter of fact, early in his life when I.K. Dairo formed a band in Ilesha, he bade his kid brother to come and lead the band which Orlando did but for a while. The stint gave the tyke a taste of leadership which prepared him for the time he was capable of being a solid leader.

With an award even though honorary, I.K. Dairo brought juju music to another milestone.

I. K. Dairo

I. K. Dairo in London

MILESTONES
DELE OJO
† INTRODUCED THE HIGHLIFE STYLE OF GUITAR PLAYING TO JUJU MUSIC

Somehow, somewhere and heavens only knows how and where, the administrative and commercial acumen of the Africans are either bankrupt or non-existent. For instance in Europe or in the west in general, if an artist, say a musician, makes a hit record, that single hit record will be so administratively nurtured and commercially packaged in such a way that in one stroke, the musician could become a millionaire. But not so with the African artist even with so many hit records. Given the population of each of the African countries, one would think that with the buying power of the Africans who reserved a special place in their souls for social occasions, the African artists would be swimming in millions of monies. But such is not the case. With the population of Nigeria invariably put at 100,000,000 to 150,000,000, shouldn't every Nigerian musician with hit records be millionaires? Sad to say not and herein comes Dele Ojo who in the 1960s had a great number of record hits but could not even get near to the shadow of being a quarter-millionaire. Barely ten years after he had been disjointed from popularity and not making much music anymore, he is still striving to make a living--as a preacher! Somehow, somewhere, something has gone wrong.

Dele Ojo was a product of I.K. Dairo's popularity. He took off in 1963 when juju came to the limelight, and brought the music to another milestone. In one of the provinces of Ondo called Ilara-Akure and ruled by the Alara of Ilara in the old Western Region of Nigeria, that was the place of his birth in 1940. It was in his elementary school days that he straightaway showed interest in music and at the age of fifteen, he became his school's band leader. In 1959, when he became a school teacher, his interest in music did not abate but increased and it was the musical gravitational force that eventually pulled him off teaching entirely and to concentrate on music when in 1961, he joined the famous Victor Olaiya's All Stars Highlife Band, as and surprisingly enough, a trumpet player. He was in this highlife band when many of his talents started to surface. In addition to blowing a horn (serving as Olaiya's second trumpeter) he sang and played the guitar which prepared him for what later brought him to fame. When juju music became popular and Olaiya's second team was disbanded leaving him jobless, Dele Ojo then formed his own band. Surprisingly, he didn't form a

highlife band and he didn't play trumpet anymore. He formed a
juju group and started singing and playing the guitar. Since juju
music is basically a rhythm music, the urge to play his trumpet
deserted him and in 1963 Dele Ojo & His "All" Star Brothers Band
was born. Originally a highlife music player, Dele Ojo brought the
highlife style of guitar playing into juju and changed the sound of
juju music. Music lovers liked his brand of juju and when his
record *I Don't Know Why She Loves Me* was released, the sale was
so great it immediately made him the "king" of juju music. Even
though he has his alter ego in Kayode Ige and Sunny Agaga, who
played similar music, yet his records after records were hits. The
decade of the sixties could as well be called Dele Ojo's decade
because his records sold in millions both at home and overseas.
Memorable were *Bouncing Bona, Enia bi aparo, Opon oye, Eni a fe
lamo, Christiana, Aiye soro, and Owo.* At home, a day never passed
without any of the Nigeria's broadcasting systems playing his
records in dozens of the media's request programs. He became
guest of and played for kings, chiefs, princes, princesses,
politicians, aristocrats, etc. Name them, he played for them all. He
became larger than life. Women fought for his affections and it
was rumored that Obas and rich people gave to him a complete set of
musical instruments as gifts. And also clothes were showered on
him by clothiers who would like him to appear in their materials.
But with all the adulation, Dele Ojo was still his down-to-earth good
self. He never needed a bodyguard. He was approachable and
ready at any hour of the day to meet with and discuss with anybody.
His manners were charming. He was foremost of the juju artists
who used the English language in their music (e.g. *I Don't Know
Why She Loves Me, Bouncing Bona, Christiana*). A tour overseas
became inevitable. He caught England by storm because all of the
Nigerian communities in Great Britain which organized dances
featuring him and his band had the dance halls all jam packed.
Repeat performances were all sell-out too. Dele Ojo whacked the
guitar with confidence. His solo work was superfluous. He could
play both the rhythm and the lead guitar effortlessly. His rhythm
section was one of the best sounding rhythm part of a band heard by
music lovers in a long time. His bassist was actually something
else. He gave him a "trade-mark" with his style of calypso-cubanos
type of bass guitar playing. When he returned from his first
England tour, he made a record about it called *Ilu Oyinbo Dara*
(England is good) extolling the life in England and also describing
the hardships of African students and their survival. Through this
record, he was the one who made parents of Nigerians studying
overseas to realize what their children go through before obtaining

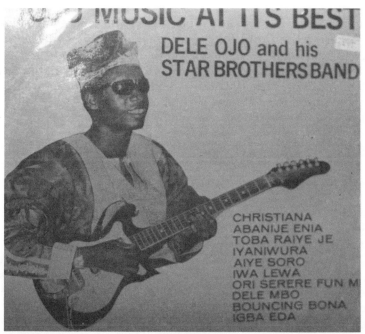

Dele Ojo

Dele Ojo standing by the church billboard

their certificates. It was such a big hit, it broke all sales records.
When the second military take-over in Nigeria came and he made
a record about the valor of Colonel Fajuyi called *Colonel Adekunle
Fajuyi*, who died very bravely to prevent a breach of trust, the record
was a big hit. With Dele Ojo, every single record he made was a hit.
He then made a tour of the United States of America and the
reception from the Nigerians was more than overwhelming, it was
a frenzy. The repeat tour of the U.S. was also great and this must
have given him the wrong impression of the day-to-day life in the
country of the almighty dollar. He decided to go back and stay for a
long time and probably for good--a big mistake! While he was
away, two juju artists emerged to fill his gap. They were Ebenezer
Obey and Sunny Ade. Meanwhile, while he was in the U.S., Dele
Ojo started to realize that things were not what they seemed to be. To
this end, his boys became home-sick, deserted him and left for
home. Secondly, when there were no nightclubs to book his type of
music, he had to survive as a nine-to-five commuter. Lastly, he was
not new to his fans anymore and the adulation was now subdue.
Eventually, he went back home.
    When Dele Ojo arrived back in Nigeria, he discovered that his
time had passed. He made an LP called *Gele Odun* and it failed
miserably in the market. He strived to revive himself but attention
had now been concentrated on some other artists, two of them, very
outstanding. "If you can't beat them, join them" as the saying goes
but Dele Ojo tried to beat them, but he couldn't; and he tried to join
them but he couldn't either. Eventually he packed it in.
    Dele Ojo, right from the beginning of his life had been a religious
man. And he was a teacher before becoming a musician. At this
time in his life, he couldn't teach anymore. Music, while not
unkind to him had no place for him in its abode anymore; so what
else? For survival, he resorted to preaching, tended to by a small
congregation at an outskirt of Lagos and today at Ibadan. Now,
whatever happened to Dele Ojo and his hit music and all the money
made out of them? Granted, the patriarch, Papa Badejo Okusanya,
owner of Badejo Sound Studio where Dele Ojo recorded some of his
hits died and the company is now near disintegration, but how about
Philips Records which Dele Ojo was contracted to and where he
made the bulk of his hit records? With all the money he made for
Philips, should he not have been sold a share of the company? As a
shareholder, without doubt, he would be enjoying his life today
without strain. How about a re-release of his old hits? Royalties
from these would definitely release him from any financial strain
he may have. Ever since Dele Ojo introduced the highlife style of

guitar playing to juju music in the 1960s, it has remained in the music and brought it to another milestone.

MILESTONES
JESUS NWANCHUKU
† FIRST NON-YORUBA TO HAVE A JUJU HIT RECORD

1st Person: "Jesus Nwanchuku!"

2nd Person: "*Je...? Jesus? ... Jesus what!?*

1st Person: "Jesus Nwanchuku."

2nd Person: " *No... No... No... I mean the name of the record.*"

1st Person: "Yes, I'm giving you the name of the record."

2nd Person: "*Jesus Nwanchuku? Hmm. You don't say.*"

1st Person: "Yes, I do say."

2nd Person: "*Who made it?*

1st Person: "Jesus Nwanchuku."

2nd Person: "*Aw come on, cut out the jokes.*"

1st Person: "I'm serious. The artist's name is Jesus Nwanchuku and the record's name is Jesus Nwanchuku."

2nd Person: "*Ha... Ha... Ha... Ha... (laughter) who the... who the hell is Jesus Nwanchuku? He's got some nerve! These Ibos...these Ibos...If one thing they've got it's some nerve! Ha... Ha... Ha... Ha... (laughter again) Geessaws Wanshuku... Ha... Ha... Ha... Ha...(laughter). Don't you see the very root of sacrilege? What a name for a music; and juju for that matter. This man ate and bellyfull and went about calling himself Jesus. Yanmirin, kalami, boranboran. The very idea. Ha... Ha... Ha... Ha... (laughter again).*

Well, it was in the 1960s at a house party in London, England. There was this hit juju record just arrived from home and everybody was going agog about it. This gentleman brought the record to the party and played it and the whole dance floor was immediately filled with wriggling bodies. When it was over, there was the cry of "encore," "encore" and it was played again the second time, and the third time and the fourth. After the fourth time, this Yoruba gentleman (2nd person in the above dialogue) asked the owner of the record (1st person), the reord's title and that was how the conversation above ensued. Because the juju music was created and had been dominated by the Yorubas, the gentleman who was making enquiries about the record (2nd person in the dialogue) couldn't bring himself to believe that such a good record could be made by a non-Yoruba. After learning the identity of the record, his mind was blown to bits.   With a mixture of surprise and bemusement, he couldn't help casting aspersions at the name of the artist but not the record. Even though some devout Christians might find the name of the artist either somewhat sacrilegious or diverting, if he had been a Yoruba, denigrating it wouldn't even have come about. And it is for this reason that another milestone was reached in juju music. Njemanze, the Ibo musician who was murdered in the 1950s by members of his band was actually not a real Ibo and the Ibos of Nigeria have been known to make good music but that was the first time an Ibo would make a hit record with juju music which was never their turf. What, if anything this confirmed, was that music is a universal language.

The 1960s was the decade of one hit artists. This started with the pop groups of Great Britain. After Jesus Nwanchuku's solitary hit record, he slipped into oblivion.

Now what made the record a hit? Jesus used accordion and fashioned his style on I.K. Dairo's--a lot of drumming and fast beat. The lyric was a combination of pidgin English and Ibo, telling about Jesus' exploits with a woman. It was a vocal call and an accordion response type of music tainted with satyr and mild physical violence with a lot of Alleluyas. All in all, the record, released on Philips label, was very good and so another milestone was reached in juju music.

MILESTONES
TUNDE NIGHTINGALE
(*Ernest Olatunde Thomas*)
† ONLY JUJU ARTIST EVER TO PLAY AND RECORD A JUJU-JAZZ NUMBER

Tunde Nightingale was not a pioneer of juju music but a very early player of the music. Of all of the juju musicians, he was the only one who always experimented with the music... without him knowing it of course (*more about Tunde in SPECIAL MENTION on Page 149*). He has played the African highlife through juju music. He has played the South American rhumba and the Cuban son musics by way of juju music and successfully too. Now get this, Tunde Nightingale has played and recorded a North American jazz tune in a mixture of juju music. A juju-jazz to be exact.

Oh yes! The American jazz takes its root from Africa but since it had gone out of Africa and become westernized with great infusion of western musical instruments, it had been an American type of music and the Africans had lost interest in it. The Americans pampered and packaged it, made it their own and made it world-wide popular.

Tunde arrived into juju music when foreign and imported musics were invading and criss-crossing Lagos. Exposure to these types of music probably caused his experimentations and versatility.

Taking his cue from Tunde King, Tunde Nightingale was basically a juju music player with no frills. He had been in the music for three-and-one-half decades doing his thing and amassing fans when in 1968 he was invited by his fans to London to come and render his services. He obliged. He had fulfilled all of his engagements and was getting ready to go home when he discovered that there were not enough funds to transport him and his boys home. An arrangement was then reached between him and the Melodisc Records Company whereby some recordings would be made by him for the company and the resulting payment would be used to defray the cost of his transportation home. He and his band arrived in the studio without any particular song in mind to record. They just played. Melodisc was looking for a good single to promote two LPs he wanted Tunde to record for him. After selecting *Agbogun Gboro* for the "A" side to project as the hit song, he then needed a tune for the "B" side -- any tune, not necessarily a good tune. It didn't take much effort on Tunde's side to hit upon one. Probably wanting a change, he commanded his drummers to give him a beat based on American thematic jazz form. That was all the needed. Before one knew it, he was singing a juju song on jazz chromatic scale. He even scatted. It was so abnormal yet so incredibly beautiful, everybody in the studio was amazed. The single was released just before the release of the first one of the two LP records that he recorded. The people that bought the single bought it for the hit side "A", little did they realize that the "B" side that they didn't care for was a history making number. The title of this number is *Ko Le Sise* meaning "he can't work" (he's lazy), on Melodisc Label. *MEL 1681. 1968.* And this was how, in adversity, Tunde Nightingale brought juju music to another milestone.

Tunde Nightingale in London

MILESTONES
SUNNY ADE
(Sunday Alade Adeniyi)
† FIRST TO INTRODUCE ORGAN IN JUJU MUSIC
AND ALSO THE SLIDE GUITAR
† FIRST TO INTRODUCE SIDE-SHOWS IN JUJU
MUSIC AND MAKE IT CONCERT-LIKE
† FIRST TO BRING JUJU MUSIC TO
INTERNATIONAL PROMINENCE

Just as the 1930s and 1940s would go down in world's history as years of wars and turbulence, so will the 1960s be remembered as the decade of music and innovation.

In Nigeria, by the nineteen sixties, juju music has become a big thing. When Dele Ojo was making waves, there were a lot of juju musicians lurking in his shadow. Sunny Ade was one of them. He had made a number of singles, majority of which were name-praising records. Their turn-overs were not that particularly impressive until when in 1967 he made *Challenge Cup 1967* and scored a big hit with it. From then on, it was non-stop with him.

As his first name implies, he must have arrived into this world at the end of a third week or thereabouts in the month of September because when he chose Sunny as his first name professionally, one might have guessed. On September 20, 1946, in Ondo in the old Western State of Nigeria (now Ondo State) Sunday Alade Adeniyi popularly known as King Sunny Ade (the King came later) was born. At the very tender age of ten, he became interested in music and not very long, he became his elementary school's band leader. As it has always been with African parents who would rather see their children study to become doctors, lawyers, engineers, or architects, Sunny's parents were no exception to the lofty but archaic idea and it was no surprise when he met with their objection of him becoming a musician. At the ripe age of eighteen years, he parted with them with the feeling that if he could not be an architect of a facade, he could at least be the architect of his own fortune as the saying goes. He arrived in Lagos ("where the action was") in 1964 and two years later in 1966, he formed his own band called, The Green Spot Band. What emerald and the magic number of 10 had in store for him, nobody and he himself included knew, but when he formed his band with 10 players, the going was not easy. Rehearsals night after night, the awesome presence of big names and established bands and their leaders, the rough and tumble nature of life in the capital city, the release of some singles that brought out no encouraging turn-overs, all were enough to deter this young man but he would not be deterred. Barely three years after his arrival, his efforts started to yield good dividends. The 1967 soccer match competition known as the Challenge Cup did it for him (*See Challenge Cup in A WHOLE SCENE GOING on Page 108*). When the record that he made in memory of the competition was brought to Mrs. Gee of the Stern's Radio Store in London's west end, she rejected it outright. Barely three days later when she realized what hit her, she was crazily ordering it in hundreds. But even at that time, Sunny Ade was not that particularly good but listening to the record attentively, evidence of a great potential was there to be discovered. Today, if one compares his music on that record to what he plays nowadays, then one will definitely nod in agreement to the above mentioned statement. The more he made recordings, the more he improved and the faster he was experimenting with some other instruments to beef-up his music. Between 1968 and 1969 he had been tagged Wizard of the Strings or as his fans would like it called "The Master Guitarist" (Alujonnu Onigita) But wait! Not so fast! There were good musicians around and fans of these musicians did not take kindly to this accolade. Ebenezer Obey who had hitherto displaced Dele Ojo was still waxing good and strong. His fans were in legions and to them, he was the greatest. Ebenezer soon became Sunny Ade's alter ego and rivalry started which raged like bellows of a cruel sea for good five years. The acrimony came to a point when it was rumored that the two of them were on war-path.

But it actually turned out that the two principals could not care less what the other was doing and it was their fans that were sowing the seeds of rancor. Exactly on Thursday the 16th of August, 1973, Sunny Ade took the initiative to dispel the rumor. Unheralded, he went to Ebenezer Obey's night spot OBE MILIKI SPOT where he found Obey playing and joined him on the stage to play some tunes to the joys and approval of the attendees who cheered and cheered and who were relieved of the tension.

Maybe Sunny Ade took his queue from Fela Kuti, the Afrobeat inventor, who had created a side-show for his music by making Miss Dele Johnson his resident dancer, however, Sunny actually went a bit further and introduced about four dancing girls as a side-show to his music--a first in juju music. Later on, the girls were discarded for men who danced and doubled as chorus singers. In this decade, keyboard was his first innovation but which didn't catch on. He later re-introduced it and it became a permanent fixture in his band. The usual one talking drum player was increased to three and these drummers became the center piece of attraction in his sound. Now, Sunny was king never mind real or imaginary, whether title won or honorary. The sound of juju through some of Sunny Ade's innovations could not now be ignored by western observers and listeners, as the decade of the nineteen eighties crept up. Two western public relations men who had listened to and seen Sunny's act definitely knew that this was something, if commercially well packaged, could land a pot of gold internationally.

They had seen that Sunny Ade was young, nimble, and could relate to college students who were liberal as far as to any point that the word could be stretched. They had found his music different, invigorating and joyful. And to this end, playing for a listening audience instead of dancing enthusiasts would be more appropriate and commercially viable; so they set to work. Before long, international audience was created and everybody wanted to know what juju music was all about. Has it anything to do with voodoo? What part of Africa did it come from? Is the exponent of it who called himself a king a real African king? Bring the music up here and let's hear it, they seemed to be saying.

Any Nigerian would have to rack his or her brain to be able to furnish information on the town where Sunday Alade Adeniyi is king but since the title had been attached to his name, it was greatly exploited and the agents did not feel any need to explain to anybody whether he was a juju king or a ruling king; and that if he was a real king, at where was he crowned but if a juju king, in which competition did he win the title. By the time he arrived in New York in the United States of America, publicity was at such fever pitch that the Americans were eager to see this African King who was such a good musician. Yes, Sunny Ade caught America by storm and juju music came to international prominence.

Sunny Ade's band was alarmingly and unnecessarily large. Alarmingly, because in usualness, juju music is played by a small group of players and unnecessarily, because he did not need five guitarists plus a slide guitarist and a synthesizer player. Good as his music was, with the exception of the bass guitar, all the five guitars, the synthesizer and the slide guitar, sounded pretty much the same. The center piece of attraction of his music were the talking drummers but did he really need three of them in addition to a conga drummer and a drum set player? There was a claves player and a maracas shaker and with four dancers doubling as chorus singers, the stage was now crowded with an almost eighteen-man band. Introducing the slide guitar and the side shows into juju were new milestones reached in the music through the efforts of Sunny Ade.

"ALUJONNU ONIGITA"

Sometimes to translate the Yoruba language to english and get its
exact meaning, becomes a hazard. Even when it is maneuvered by
having its statement transpositioned, then the risk of losing the
meaning in translation becomes present. Worse still, some words,
names or statements in Yoruba have no direct, exact or equivalence
in meaning in the english language. When Sunny Ade's fan, who
marveled at the extraordinary way he plays the guitar wanted to
show their appreciation by giving him an alias that signifies the
acme of perfection, they dubbed him "ALUJONU ONIGITA."
When this is translated to english as "THE MASTER
GUITARIST," it loses its meaning completely even though it makes
its point. Alujonnu in Yoruba folklore is a troll, demon, apparition,
fairy, genie or any unusual being that is capable of performing
extraordinary things and whose place of abode is usually forests,
jungle caves, hills, mountains etc., etc. But simply because this
creature performs extraordinary things, is it then a master?
    Guitar is an invention of the west, and the Yorubas have no name
for it. They call it gita. But similar looking instruments made in
Nigeria called goje and molo are abound. The Yoruba word onigita
actually means owner of a guitar, in english. Atagita is much
closer to the english word guitarist; and the word master in Yoruba
is olori or oga. Now to translate Alujonnu Onigita (the demon who
possesses a guitar) as Master guitarist (Oga ata molo) is way off the
actual translation. Even guitar genius which could have been a
near appropriate translation is still short of the point.
    Ebenezer Obey was caught in nearly the same situation when his
band broke up and he had to reform the band and weed out some
internal dissenters. After reforming the band, he renamed it Inter
Reformers Band probably to let people know that the internal
dissention that plagued the band is over and that he has reformed a
new one. That was a good effort but members of a broken group that
is reformed or regrouped are hardly known as reformers. The word
reformer has a very different meaning to it.
    Example: Years ago during the colonial days in Lagos, the
colonial government built a house in Isheri, on the outskirts of
Lagos called Isheri Reform Home, where hard-core juvenile delin-
quents were taken to, to be retracted, reprogrammed, and well
packaged before being returned to normal decent society. This was
known as reformation and graduates of an institution like this
were known as reformers. The Isheri Reform Home was like a
penitentiary for these louts, truants, miscreants and deviants. The
institution authorities not only strive to make them penitent by

being tough on them but trained them in various trades before
sending them back to their homes. The Isheri boys in the old days
were known for their toughness and their boxing team, coached by
Red Raymond, a famous Nigerian Lightweight boxer, always
produced Olympic stars. If Obey reformed his band without
reformers, Inter Reformers was hardly a name to give to the new
band. Yes, Obey understood what he meant when he chose the name
but it was another instance when word or statement lost its meaning
in translation, or failed to convey an intended meaning.

Sunny Ade

SPECIAL MENTION

★ TOGO LAWSON

(Akinwale Lawson)
(RIP)

One of the pioneers of Juju music was Togo Lawson, a dramatic character. Born in Lagos at No. 2 Evans Street, his father was a native of the neighboring country of Togoland but his mother was a Nigerian from the town of Ijebu Ode who by profession was a hair-braider. She subsidized her income by selling Taba (powdered tobacco leaves).

Togo Lawson's real name was Akinwale Lawson. A jolly fellow, he was always seen playing the tambourine and singing mostly in the night to amuse people --children especially. He loved kiddies.

He attended St. John's Aroloya School for kindergarten and then proceeded to Holy Cross Catholic School for primary where he graduated. After graduating from primary school, he joined the army and served with the Royal West African Frontier Force (RWAFF) in the World War II. He came back home from the war with brain problem because from this time on, his behavior was somewhat erratic. His hair-style was always the military type "short back and sides" and he was always in his khaki army shirt leaving its epaulets and cover pockets unbuttoned all flapping as he pounded or slapped on the tambourine. On this musical instrument, he was superb.

After the World War II, he joined the Nigerian Railways as a handyman. In the night, he continued to sing and to play the tambourine in the streets coming all the way from Evans Street and turning to Odunfa Street walking up to Tokunboh Street. At Tokunboh Street, he sometimes turned left towards Oshodi Street or at times turned right to Massey Street and walked towards Ita Faji market. During this tenure at the Nigerian Railways, the first General Strike of Workers in Nigeria which lasted 44 days in Lagos and 52 days at the out-stations of Nigeria commenced on June 21st, 1945 in Lagos. Togo Lawson composed a song about the strike which was a big hit but was never recorded. People loved to sing the song which went:

1)   *The oil seller is shouting; the beans are cooked and well done*
      The salt seller is shouting; the beans are cooked and well done
      Railways is shouting; we refused to go back to work
      Zappas is shouting; we refused to go back to work

Odunfa Street

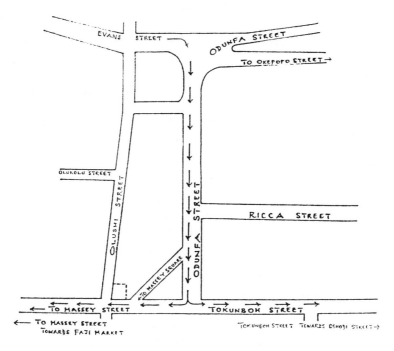

Togo's route

The white bosses thought we were stupid
They laid us off
They refused to pay us our bonus
We refused to go back to work

2)   *You slept without thinking*
     Then the ants have not bitten into you
     The termites have not bitten into you
     (worms) have not bitten into you
     Railway is shouting; the beans are cooked and well done
     Zappas is shouting; the beans are cooked and well done
     The oil seller is shouting; the beans are cooked and well done
     The salt seller is shouting; the beans are cooked and well done
     The white boss thought we were stupid
     They laid us off
     They refused to pay us our bonus.
     We refused to go back to work.

He also composed some other famous songs including *Sergeant Major Stoukas, The gap-toothed pretty petite girl, and Elemu* (the Palmwine tapper).   When the strike was over, he never went back to work.   He switched to guitar when he formed his juju group. Through heavy cigarette smoking he became sick.   He was taken to Ijebu for treatment where he died in the late 1940s.   He was about 48 years old when he died. He never recorded any of his songs.

SPECIAL MENTION

★ 'TUNDE NIGHTINGALE
(RIP)

The French words "*niht*"-night and "*galan*"-to sing or yell, make up the word nightingale which for that particular reason is the name of a bird. The nightingale is a bird of Europe which makes its annual migration to Africa as a matter of must dictated by nature. A bird, is a bird, is a bird; but not so with the nightingale. What then makes the nightingale different?. At sundown when all the birds have given it a rest, the nightingale keeps singing and it sings all night. So far for the bird and its name.

Some years after juju music started in Lagos, a young man by the name of Ernest Olatunde Thomas started playing the music and formed his own group. On one particular social occasion when he was called upon to render his musical services, this admirer of his who had been dancing to his music decided to partially call it off by midnight and took a nap. When he woke up way past midnight he was surprised to see merriment still abound with music still in the air. Upon checking the supplier of the music, he was surprised to see that it was nobody else but Tunde. He then said to him that he didn't only sound beautiful but he sang like a nightingale. The name stuck and thus overnight, Olatunde Thomas became 'Tunde Nightingale.

Of all the Nigerian juju music makers, none was and is as versatile as Tunde Nightingale. A guitarist, he started playing the music two or three decades after the music surfaced in Lagos. Imported music like calypso, son, rumba, jazz etc., etc, that were around at that time probably made him to vary his guitar playing style but basically he remained a juju artist. When 'Tunde talked, he was like any other human being but when he sang, he was different. The disparity between his speaking and singing voices was so great that nobody who heard Tunde spoken in his tenor voice would believe he was the owner of the sonorous but high-pitched singing voice. Ever nice and jolly, he had legion of admiring fans who always bought his records whether hit or not. He was never out of popularity not just because he had a charismatic name nor because he had built a name for himself over the years but because once in a while he came up with a hit record. The 1960s was a case in point when new artists particularly Dele Ojo and Kayode Ige dominated the music scene with their hit records and out of nowhere, Tunde came up with a record called *Sekere Alafin* and beat them all to the top of the "chart." And talking about versatility, he was versatility at its most amazing. In addition to juju his specialty, he could play highlife, calypso, son (GV), rhumba and believe it or not jazz. Jazz? Yes, jazz and no kidding. As a matter of fact he released a juju-jazz single *Kole Sise* (He cannot work or he's lazy), (He's a sloth) in the late sixties in adversity.

Going to London to perform around that time was in fashion and he too decided to go having been invited. He actually completed his engagements without a hitch when, as preparation to come back home was well under way, he discovered one morning that he was stranded. Either through bad management or lack of finesse on the part of his PR man and road manager, funds for transportation back home for him and his boys were lacking. Being a popular artist, like lightning, news of this misfortune reached Lagos and a newspaper actually displayed a front-page picture of him walking on the streets of London's Leicester Square near Piccadilly Circus with a bold head-line that read "TUNDE NIGHTINGALE STRANDED IN LONDON." But 'Tunde took everything in stride by simply smiling in the picture. A way out however was found. Mrs. Cecil Gee who co-owned STERN'S RADIOS (located near Warren Street underground train station) with her relative Mr. Martine, was familiar with Tunde's music. A buff of African music, she usually sold his records in large numbers in her stores. When Tunde's problem reached her, she was the first person to believe that his problem was no problem. Ade Bashorun, formerly of the Ambrose Campbell's West African Rhythm Brothers, then a staff at Melodisc Records, set the owner of the recording company in motion. Cecil Gee assured Emile Shalit that if ever he took on the problems of Tunde, he would hit a gold mine. From Lagos, the green light from EMI and Jofabro Records companies of which Tunde was contracted, was given to Shalit, owner of the Melodisc Records to record Tunde, proceeds of which could be slated for his transportation home. Shalit smelt gold and he immediately arranged a recording session in Maximum Sound Studio at Old Kent Road which he co-owned with Vic Keary the manager and chief recording engineer.

Tunde and his boys arrived at the studio without any compositions and started recording impromptu. He had recorded tunes in juju, highlife, rhumba, and son but Shalit wanted more so as to have a wide range of choice for the best of two albums he wanted. All of a sudden, Tunde turned to Jazz!, with juju flavor. Everybody was pleasantly stunned. Mrs. Gee who had earlier expressed her pleasure in meeting with Tunde in the flesh, and who had been tapping her feet to the beat of all of 'Tunde's numbers flipped with delight.

When the first of the two LPs came out, Flash Domincii of the West African Supersonics was the first person to bring a handful few to Nigeria for late Papa Badejo Okusanya. When he distributed the handful to the stores, they were all sold out in only one day. The EMI immediately contacted Melodisc for the Nigerian release. This took effect, and the sale was great. Tunde was able to come back home in triumph with his image untarnished.

His juju-jazz could be described as a milestone because the record, released as a single, even though was not popular, no other juju musician tried juju-jazz after his. A special mention should be made of this very popular gentleman because he gave his all to juju music. Tunde died in the nineteen-eighties. His music lives forever. Rest In Peace.

SPECIAL MENTION

★ JOFABRO
Joseph Olajoyegbe Fajimolu

The record business, maybe because of the amount of money that is so much involved in it, becomes attractant of speculators, hard-core bargainers and devil-may-care brief-case carrying quasi entrepreneurs. Its lucrative seemingness also inducted into its magnetic field people who hasn't the foggiest notion of what a sound constitutes but would like to make bigger and quicker bucks.

In any business where there is throat-cutting, rat-racing, backslapping, politicking, etc., etc., therein can also be found some people who are forthright, upright, and unadulterated.

In the early days of disc making and its related business in Nigeria, involved were countries like France, Britain and Germany which hadn't a clue about how to reach the core of the natives. Soon, a company known as Angard was formed. ANGARD was the acronym for Association of Nigeria Gramophone and Record Dealers. Members of ANGARD included illustrious Nigerian names like late Badejo Okunsanya, Shiwoku, Oyenkwelu and the still living A.O. L. Araba. Before a sigh of relief could be heard, it was discovered that ANGARD was copper-tight and its mantle of exclusively with regards to membership unpenetrated let alone shattered. Then something happened; a turn-about. A gentleman by the name of Joseph Olajoyegbe Fajimolu who hailed from Ilesha, moved his base from Ogbomosho to Lagos in 1948. On August 1st, 1948, he joined Houghtons West Africa Ltd., at 78 Victoria Street as a clerical assistant. Two years later in 1950, he left. Why did he leave? Well, even though he could not read a note of music, he liked music and wanted to get into its business aspects. He opened a store on 21 Balogun Street as a record retailer. Innocent, forthright and undirectional minded, he put in an application to join ANGARD. ANGARD was representing DECCA through the agency of a gentleman in Accra, Gold Coast (now Ghana) by the name of Major Kinder. Some other companies that were also being represented were the EMI, Parlophone, etc. While waiting to hear from ANGARD, an event took place. The nation of Nigeria was making history. It had elected its Lagos City's first black and Nigerian Mayor ever in the person of Dr. Ibiyinka Olorun-Nimbe who had gone on a visit to Britain. The Mayor was returning to Lagos from this visit in an oceanliner when in the Atlantic, the ship was being followed by a probably disoriented pilot sperm-whale. Mistaken for a killer whale which might constitute a danger to the ship, the whale was either shot or its body accidentally ripped by the ship's propeller. Anyway, the whale died and was washed ashore on the Lagos Bar Beach. Heaven knows who spread the rumor that when a slice from the body of this fish was cut off, it immediately replicated itself, hundreds of Lagosians, day and night, thronged the beach to either have a look at this wonderful fish or have a slice of its flesh. A young musician by the name of Adeolu Akinsanya who had just arrived in Lagos from the up-country and who had just formed his band with a type of music called Agidigbo decided to make his first ever recording with a song based on this event called *Abunbutan Eja Mayor* (Unlimited cuts. The Mayor's fish). He recorded the song on Badejo label. Anxious to hear how he and his band sounded on a record disc, he was advised to go to the stores of Joseph to listen to his newly released record. That was his first meeting with Olajoyegbe which resulted in a good business association and wonderful personal friendship that beautifully endured.

Back to Olajoiyegbe and ANGARD. For a long time, Olajoyegbe did not hear from ANGARD and when it finally dawn on him that he wasn't wanted in this group, he started to write overseas for an agency of his own. At this time, unknown to him (Olajoiyegbe), ANGARD was having problems with Major Kinder and it has resulted in a split of which ANGARD's agency was revoked and its members disbanded. One of Joseph Olajoyegbe's letters overseas was to Polydor Records in London. The company directed Olajoyegbe to Major Kinder in Accra who wrote and gave Olajoyegbe the agency that he took away from ANGARD. Major Kinder later came to Nigeria to meet with and to have a face-to-face discussion with his new man and also to have some contract signed. The first recording of the new agency took place at the NBC studios and the recording engineer was one Mr. Bannister. Now, all the displaced and ex-Angard members started to apply for membership of the new agency of Olajoyegbe's whom they have once snubbed. What a twist of fate! With a man of lesser spirit, these men would have been paid back in their own coins but Olajoyegbe took them all back. No questions asked. What a human being! He must be a special man deserving special mention.

Now, has Olajoyegbe any contribution to juju music? Oh yes! Mention his name and some people would ask Ola.....who? But mention the acronym he used for the name of his recording company JOFABRO and a lot of people will say Ah-a-a-a! yes, I know him. And this acronym came to him by chance. He did not choose it by himself.

Apart from other types of music like agidigbo, apala, sakara, highlife, etc., some of whose players, big recording companies wouldn't even touch, Olajoyegbe has recorded great names in juju music like Tunde Nightingale, Ojoge Daniel, I.K. Dairo and Fatayi Olagunju popularly known as Fatayi Rolling Dollar.

He has stepped in to patch-up a rift but unsuccessfully between Fatayi Rolling Dollar and Ebenezar Obe when Obe was a drummer and back-up singer in Fatayi's group. All the artists that recorded on his JOFABRO label got generous royalties and were treated well. They have all made name-praising recordings of him, the biggest hit of which was Adeolu's that went thus:

The gull (Lekeleke), save me
The dove (eiye Adaba), save me
I hurried to the Ifa (oracle) forest
I struggled at the base of the palm-tree
The palm-tree shook, I thought it was raining
I was starving to death one day
But for compassionate, a native of Ilesha
He gave me two eko mounds (corn) , I ate one
At sundown, I ate the other
Thank you, Josy Ola
The son of Olatunji
The son of Olaniran
The son of Olajoyegbe
The son of his mother at Oke Odan
You can't bear relation to a person
And put imposition on that person
You have journeyed to the peak of seniority
You have torn the outfit on me
The son of his mother at Oke Odan
The person I see is Josy, and I like him
The person, the person I see is Josy , and I like him
You won't die, you won't decompose, you won't end-up eating
    bone after meat (meaning you won't end up in misery)
The person,the person I see is Josy, and I like him.

SPECIAL MENTION

★ SEIGNEURIAL RIGHT, THE HAUSAS AND THE COLONIAL GOVERNMENT

Barely was Lagos ceded to the British by King Dosunmu of Lagos on August 6, 1861, when it started to have its first problem with the Lagos's landed property. A group of native fishermen that had hitherto formed themselves into an association known as the IDEJOS (landowners) claimed that Lagos was not the property of Dosunmu and he had no right to give it away.

Six months and twenty-four days later on February 11, 1862, the British backed off. Through the then Governor of Lagos, Consul Henry Stanhope Freeman, the British issued a notice to assure the Idejos that cession of Lagos should not be construed as seizure of their landed property. There and then, the Idejos agreed but skeptically to the treaty of the cession.

But did the British really back off? No, not really. Early in June of 1912, the Colonial Office in Downing Street, London, under Lord Harcourt as Secretary of State for the colonies, passed a law that gave the colonial government in all of its West African Dependences the right to use the natives' land for its purpose but to pay the deprived owners a type of compensation known as "Seigneurial Right"--Seigneurial pronounced sa-nyur`i-al. What does seigneurial mean? Simply, it means: Held by feudal tenure. This compensation was later found to be a disappointing pittance. (*Read Oluwa Landcase, Page 49*).

The Northern Nigeria was where this law first took hold and the colonial government got away with it. The Hausas of Northern Nigeria had always been religious, autocratic, laid-back and with that attitude of having somebody doing things for them and they in return just paying for the services. Also, they have this morbid affinity for things British and white with the belief that the British were all-in-all and cold do no wrong. And so, favoritisms for the British were boundless. Now, one would think that with the enjoyment of all these favors, the British would immediately come to the defense of the Hausas should an occasion warranted it. Not so; but on the contrary the British always spared no effort to ridicule or poke fun at the Hausas for whatever it was worth. There have been many instances but only three need be mentioned.

1) On June 29, 1921, the Emir of Katsina who upon arrival in Liverpool, was going about barefooted with an European Resident of the Northern Provinces of Nigeria. For days, the fun and ridicule of this Mohammedan ruler in the England papers continued. The British public was made to know that he was a Hausa, a ruler, a Northern Nigerian and a Mohammedan. With the headline, "The Barefooted Emir" over his picture, the ridicule continued unabated. Fortunately Herbert Macaulay, the thorn-in-the-flesh of the colonial government was in London at the time to deal with Oluwa Landcase. In a series of press conferences, he lashed out at the thoughtless action on the part of those responsible for the health and safety of the Emir or of the Emir himself. If an European was travelling with him as an adviser and this white person did not see it fit to take the climate as a first consideration, then he would be held responsible if anything should happen to the Emir, warned Macaulay. After Macaulay's warning, the jokes and ridicule instantly stopped, and the Emir was supplied with a pair of beautiful boots which he used for the rest of his stay in England and his subsequent pilgrimage to Mecca and back to Northern Nigeria, his native land.

2) In the 1950s, a Northern delegation to a constitutional conference in London included an enlightened Emir. It was during the cold season and the Emir was very cold indeed. In the British tradition, he was advised that a cup of tea would warm him up and the Emir accepted this cup of tea gracefully. Even though the tea went some way, it did not go far enough to drive the cold away so he requested for another cup. The second cup still did not make it. Eyebrows started raising when there was an indication for a request of a third one; then something happened. The tea server was instructed to go and boil a big pot of tea and to keep filling the Emir's tea-cup, immediately the Hausa gentleman gulped down the preceding tea. Not only that, he was given specific instructions to count how many cups of tea the Emir consumed. Unaware that it was a set-up, the innocent Northern Nigerian gentleman continued to drink up the teas as his cup was being filled and praising the "generosity and hospitality" of the British. In the African tradition, one never recoils at a hospitality or generosity, but the Emir did not know that this did not obtain in every situation or country.

Anyway, for the duration of the conference that lasted between one to two hours, the ruler consumed 47 cups of tea. It was the biggest joke and ridicule in the following day British newspapers. Firstly, they did not even allow this man to leave their country before starting to make fun of him and secondly they did not fail in their "duty" to let the public know that he was a Hausa, a Northern

The Northerners
Northerners on horses participating in Durbar

Nigerian and a ruler. When the jokes continued unabated, it them drew fire from the West African Students in Britain who per chance had discovered that the Emir was set-up. There and then, the derision stopped!

3) After World War II, France was slipping away as a world power. To prove that it was still a force to be reckoned with, it manufactured its atomic bomb and decided to test its efficacy by the early 1960s. Now, guess where General Charles de Gaulle had the gall to test his country's weapon of destruction--the Sahara desert!

Panic gripped the African countries particularly those South of the Sahara. The African scientists alerted France to the risk of human lives but France couldn't bulge. There were protests all over the world and songs by juju and highlife music artists in Nigeria and other parts of Africa asking France not to do it but deGaulle couldn't care less because he felt he had a stake in Africa and its colony was where he wanted to do the test. The street demonstrations forced the then Prime Minister of Nigeria, Alhaji Sir Abubakar Tafawa Balewa to travel to Britain to see Sir Harold McMillan in order to get McMillan to talk de Gaulle out of this test. Why Britain and why Tafawa Balewa? Firstly, the Nigerians felt that since the country was once under British rule, rapport would be easier as friend to friend and also since Britain and France were world powers, good rapport would be easier to achieve as a world power to a world power. Secondly , since Alhaji Sir Abubakar Tafawa Balewa was a Hausa from the Northern Nigeria where the British had enjoyed great favors during the colonial days, he would be able to get through to the British Prime Minister in a face to face discussion, so thought the Nigerian public. But it was a big mistake and Sir Abubakar regretted making this trip. When he arrived in Britain, the reason for his visit was not newsworthy anymore to the British newspapers. What they seized upon was the frightened look on the "ugly" face of the Hausa man that bore a tribal slash from the bridge of his nose to the base of his jaw. When the joke continued without an end in sight, then the West African students with a powerful union in Britain threatened to insult the Queen! Now, now, now, now, this must not be allowed to happen.... and the jokes instantly stopped.

McMillan told Balewa that it was a pipe dream to think that Britain would wage war against France because of Nigeria. And as for sanctions, he might as well forget that because Britain would not put any sanctions on France. Now what would Britain do? Nothing.

The Nigerian Prime Minister came home disgusted and promised himself never ever again to cave-in to any public outrage over a matter of which a negative result of it had been known to him beforehand.

However, the British assured Nigeria that it would construct a contrivance on Nigeria's boarder which would arrest any fall-outs resulting from the explosion. Ha! What an assurance!

On February 13, 1960, France exploded its atomic weapon in the Sahara Desert and the wind carried its fall-outs to many African countries. In Nigeria, there was a great pandemic of stupor, convulsion, dizziness, severe vomiting and flu. A lot of Africans were victims including this writer. It was a big shame.

Now let us come to the Hausas themselves. They drove the rest of Nigeria to the edge of lunacy by their ridiculous often embarrassing hankering for anything British and they have on occasions drew unkind exchanges from the rest of Nigeria. A case in point was what happened in Nigeria in the later part of the 1950s.

To test the ability of Nigerians at governing themselves, the British first introduced regional self government with a central head. The Hausas with their related minority tribes were given a Northern Regional Government and a Hausa Premier with a British Colonial Governor. The Ibos of the East and the Yorubas of the Western Nigeria were also given the same. The Central ruling was concentrated in Lagos, with a Federal Government, a Nigerian Prime Minister and a British Colonial Governor General.

Immediately the Yorubas of the West attained this regional self rule, its Premier, Chief Obafemi Awolowo fired Sir John Rankine the white British Colonial Governor of the Western Region and made Oba (king) Adesoji Aderemi, the Oni of Ife, a black, a Nigerian, an African and a natural ruler, its Governor--a first in Africa and on the face of the earth. This drew fire from the rest of the two regions. Criticism from the Ibos in the East was more mundane. They charged that the West was dragging Nigerian respected natural rulers into politics and politics is a dirty game. Criticism from the Hausas of the North was more than laughable, it was asinine. The North charged that West had committed treason against the white "benefactor." But when congratulatory messages from all over the world started to pour in on the action of the West and the whole thing seemed to be working, the East, followed suit. Dr. Nnamdi Azikiwe, the Premier of the East, fired Sir Hugo Marshall, the white British Governor of the Eastern Region and replaced him with a black Ibo man Dr. Francis Ibiam. By now everybody thought the North would do same but before one knew it, the Hausas came out with a statement that the Colonial Governor of the North was not going to be asked to resign his job. Left with Sir Brian Sherwood-Smith the British Colonial Governor of the North, he was ready to quit since his two good friends in the "On Her Majesty's Service" had gone but he was left in the embarrassing position of quitting on the Queen of England and serving in the midst of two black governors who would make him comfortable.

Nigeria became divided on this issue with the North on one side against the rest of Nigeria on the other side. Cruel exchanges started flying and tongue lashing was hitting the Hausas like missiles from all parts of Nigeria until the North caved-in and Alhaji Ahmadu Bello the Sardauna of Sokoto, Premier of the then Northern Region of Nigeria, booted Sir Brian Sherwood-Smith and replaced him with the enlightened and very educated Hausa man the Emir of Kano.

If the North were suffering from psychosis and neurosis simultaneously, its attachment to the British could not be that much ridiculous but such was the morbid affinity.

Emir with staff

SPECIAL MENTION

MUSULUMI
1775-1780
★ THE MUSLIM (MOSLEM) RELIGION
★ MOHAMEDANISM VERSUS FETISH

Babaluwaiye, Obatala, Orunmila, Sango, Yemoja, Ifa, Esu or Elegba, Ogun etc, these were some of the idols that the people who inhabited Lagos from Ile-Ife worshipped. The religion, known as idolatry or paganism was brought with them from Ile-Ife and at some points interwove with their professions of herbalism, cultism and extra-sensory perception. The paganistic Lagos revelled in this until in the 1770s when a change seemed to be in the making.

The first imported or foreign religion surfaced around this time during the reign of King Adele Ajosun between 1775-1780. It was the Muslim religion.

The Muslim religion came to Nigeria before any other foreign religion but problem was, it found itself unable to be well rooted. It didn't offer anything more than morality and total belief in Allah the great, the merciful, the compassionate. Anything outside this was materialistic and should be shunned as taught by the religion. Maybe if it had come with a promise or offers of human needs and improvements as did the other religion, Christianity, that came after it and had massive converts, it would have been more accepted beginning from Lagos.

The first sign of problem for the religion however came from the King's palace. King Adele Ajosun was an Ifa oracle worshiper. He always made weekly sacrifice before the Ifa oracle and he was loved by his subjects even though some of the elders were not pagans. But not long, things started changing and the Oba started to lose support of the elders. The Oba's children, bent on asserting their own rights introduced Egungun from the palace. The egugun masquerade was fetish and the elders felt that it was an abomination that smacked right in the face of the dignity of the highly respected King particularly when the Mohamendan religion was taking its hold in the country. If this seemed like an incident that could be resolved amicably, it was not because war eventually broke out and at a certain point the Oba had to go into exile after suffering defeat. He later regained his throne but died two years after this. He reigned from 1775-1780.

Muslims at prayers

HISTORY OF JUJU MUSIC

CHRONOLOGY

.....1900s—1980s
ROOTS OF JUJU MUSIC

decade after decade, graduation in elements, instrumentation and style came to juju music.

1 ???.....1900s—1920s *Minstrels*

1. Tambourine
2. Samba drum

...a music, with no particular name to it, started in Lagos with minstrels playing tambourine or samba drum.

2 1920s—*Duos and Combos*

1. Tambourine
2. Samba drum
3. Banjo or guitar or ukulele or mandoline (string instruments)
4. Sekere

...a decade later, its instrumentations included strings and sekere.

3 1930s—*Ensembles*

1. Tambourine
2. Samba drum
3. String instruments
4. Sekere
5. Triangle

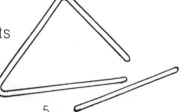

5

...*one more instrument, the triangle, was added the following decade and in the decade the music got a name to it. It was called "Juju".*

4 1940s—*Bands*
(Numbers 2 and 5 eliminated)

1. Tambourine
3. String instruments (electric guitar)
4. Sekere
6. Cowbells
7. Gangan (talking drum)
8. Conga drums
9. Bongos
10. Claves

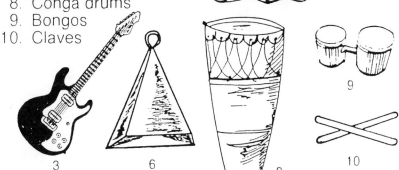

...forty years later, electric guitar replaced strings and five more instruments were added.

5 1950s—*Bands*

1. Tambourine
3. String instruments (electric guitar)
4. Sekere
6. Cowbells
7. Gangan (talking drum)
8. Conga drums
9. Bongos
10. Claves
11. Agidigbo
12. Maraccas

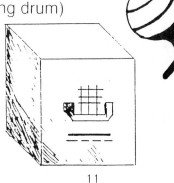

12

11

...in the 1950s, two new instruments were added making a total of invariably ten or twelve.

6 1960s—*Bands*
(Numbers 1 and 11 were also eliminated)

3. Electric guitars (Banjo, ukulele, and mandoline became obsolete)
4. Sekere
6. Cowbells
7. Gangan (talking drum)
8. Conga drums
9. Bongos (with or without)
10. Claves
12. Maraccas
13. Accordion

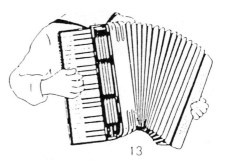

13

...in the 1960s accordion was added.

7 1970s—*Bands*
(Number 4 eliminated) (13, with or without)

3. Electric guitars
6. Cowbells
7. Gangan (talking drum)
8. Conga drums
9. Bongos (with or without)
10. Claves
12. Maraccas
14. Organ
15. Drum set

14

15

...in the 1970s drum set and organ were added.

8 1980s—*Bands*
(Number 14 eliminated) (9, 13 and 15 with or without)

3. Electric guitars
6. Cowbells
7. Gangan
8. Conga drums
9. Bongos
10. Claves
12. Maraccas
16. Slide guitar

16

...in the 1980s slide guitar was added.

EPILOGUE

OBA MEWA, IGBA MEWA – Ten kings, ten periods. This is a popular saying among the Yorubas of Nigeria. The philosophy behind it, that no king reigns for ever, holds true when one takes a look at the history of juju music. During the formative stages of juju groups, group leaders such as Alabi Labilu and Ladipo Eshugbayi were household names. When it seemed as if they would be popular for ever, out surfaced Harbor Giant and Ajayi "Koboko" and the period of the preceding celebrated leaders came to an end. The time that was marked with milestones arrivals in the music was dominated by Tunde King and Akanbi Ege but after the World War II, Ayinde Bakare and Tunde Nightingale took over in popularity. African awareness and Nigerianization brought I. K. Dairo and his own time was shared with nobody until Dele Ojo and Kayode Ige arrived at the scene. Dele Ojo soon became undisputed star of the music but in time, his reign came to an end when Ebenezer Obey and Sunny Ade started a rivalry that was to last over a decade. As these two great artists are now waning in popularity, Shina Peters, Ayinde Barrister and Kolington are stepping in their shoes.

Juju music's sound of today would make its departed pioneers turn in their graves. Variations on the music started in 1960 and today its original form is nearly obscure. More is yet to befall it because the day-to-day invention of electronic gadgets surfacing on the markets incessantly is an inducement to experimenting by young juju music players who would like to carve a name on the music's wall or to be the next to reach another milestone in the music. What have yet to be introduced into it however are horns. If this should come to pass, what would the music be called? Jujusennet? Hornsyjuju? or what? Maybe to keep it strictly juju has been why its players have not tried to delve into this "wild blue yonder." Anyway, the music has made the Nigerians happy because it has transcended tribes and tongues. What's more, it has brought the name of the country more to international prominence than the oil and has inadvertently done the job of the politicians for them more efficiently. Thank you juju. Long may your sound reign.

This is T. Ajayi Thomas saying "so long now."